James Geddes Craighead

The Story of Marcus Whitman

Early Protestant Missions in the Northwest

James Geddes Craighead

The Story of Marcus Whitman
Early Protestant Missions in the Northwest

ISBN/EAN: 9783742809995

Manufactured in Europe, USA, Canada, Australia, Japa

Cover: Foto ©ninafisch / pixelio.de

Manufactured and distributed by brebook publishing software (www.brebook.com)

James Geddes Craighead

The Story of Marcus Whitman

THE

STORY OF MARCUS WHITMAN

EARLY PROTESTANT MISSIONS IN THE NORTHWEST

BY THE

REV. J. G. CRAIGHEAD, D.D.

PRESBYTERIAN BOARD OF PUBLICATION AND
SABBATH-SCHOOL WORK, PHILADELPHIA, 1895

COPYRIGHT, 1895, BY
THE TRUSTEES OF THE PRESBYTERIAN BOARD
OF PUBLICATION AND SABBATH-
SCHOOL WORK.

PREFACE.

THE incentive to this volume was the wish to vindicate the characters and the work of the early Protestant missionaries in Oregon from aspersions which have been cast upon them; to show the importance of their labors in the development and settlement of the country; and to prove that it was through their public-spirited and patriotic services that a large part of the Northwest territory was secured to the United States.

The settlement of Oregon by any organized system began in the year 1834, when Christians in the Eastern States were induced, by the earnest desire of the Indians of the far West for the Bible and religious instruction, to take active measures to provide them with religious teachers. As soon as practicable, missionaries were sent and mission stations established among them. The influence and example of the missionaries not only promoted a Christian civilization among the Indians, but also laid the foundation of orderly and law-abiding communities wherever they labored. Their coming opened the way for the pioneer settlers of the country; and their stations formed a rallying point for American immigrants who were yearly attracted in large numbers from our Western States, and who afterward obtained ascendency in the new State.

Nor is it beyond the facts in the case to say, as did

Judge Boise in his address before the Pioneer Association of Oregon, that "history will record that these holy men were the nucleus around which has been formed and built the State of Oregon." They were "men who knew how to plant in the virgin soil the seeds of virtue and knowledge, and cultivate them as they germinated and grew into churches, schools and colleges."

Though the results of Protestant missions among the Indians in Oregon, owing to the peculiarly hostile conditions they had to encounter, were not all that the friends of the cause had at first expected, yet the presence and labors of the missionaries at this time were all important, and their effects are still felt in the religion, civilization and education which they introduced and zealously fostered.

In the preparation of this volume I have, as far as possible, availed myself of all known authorities contemporaneous with the facts discussed. Owing to the protracted controversy which has been waged respecting some of the events narrated, a more exhaustive examination was required than would otherwise have been necessary. In every such instance I have striven to be honest and impartial in the testimony adduced.

The author will feel amply repaid, if his search for the truth of history shall lead to a more general appreciation of the characters and services of the first Protestant missionaries of the far West.

WASHINGTON, D. C.

CONTENTS.

CHAPTER I.
                                                   PAGE.

Spain, France, Russia, Great Britain and the United States claim title—First three withdraw—United States claim the country by right of discovery and cession—Long controversy with Great Britain—Finally settled in 1872.................... 9

CHAPTER II.

Lewis and Clark's exploration from the Missouri river to the Columbia, in 1805-6—Valuable knowledge obtained—Government promotes the settlement of the territory............. 16

CHAPTER III.

Missouri and Pacific Fur Companies—Expeditions by sea and land—Astoria and other posts occupied—Loss of ship Tonquin—Pacific Fur Company prosperous—War with Great Britain—Fear of capture of fort, fur and supplies—Sale to North West Company by Mr. Astor's agents—Inglorious ending of his company—Treachery charged.............. 21

CHAPTER IV.

The North West Company—Its origin, explorations and repressive policy—The Hudson Bay Company, its charter rights and its power—Bloody conflicts with the North West Company—The two united with increased power—Destruction of all rival traders—Indians kept in barbarism—Opposition to all civilized settlement of the country 31

CHAPTER V.

Indians seeking the Bible—Response of churches—Methodist missionaries—Mission of the American Board—Journey to the Columbia river—Kind reception—Stations selected—Reinforcements—Success among Indians—Jesuit missionaries—Conflicting interests.................................... 41

CHAPTER VI.

The missions prosperous—Hudson Bay Company's policy to occupy the country—Americans resist it—Dr. Whitman visits Washington to save Oregon—His perilous winter ride—Arrival at Washington—Interviews with President Tyler and leading statesmen—He renders important service—Unwise claims of his friends.................................... 58

CHAPTER VII.

Dr. Whitman's visit to Boston—Return to Oregon with nearly one thousand immigrants—Services as guide and physician—Oregon saved to the United States by this large immigration—American and Hudson Bay policies conflict—Hostility shown to Americans and Protestant missionaries—Acts and motives misrepresented—Sickness among Indians—Massacre of Dr. Whitman and others............................ 74

CHAPTER VIII.

Prolonged paper discussion over the massacre—Agent Ross Browne's report—A valuable Senate document—Roman Catholic writers assail and deny its statements—Try to vindicate the conduct of their priests—In so doing, make serious charges against Protestant missionaries—Defense of the latter—Their good character and usefulness shown.............. 86

CHAPTER IX.

Wisdom and honesty of Protestant missionaries impugned—Their alleged promises to pay Indians for land—Scandals proven false—Their work depreciated on the ground that the Indians were not improved—Vindicated by the facts—Important results of Protestant missions.......................... 102

CHAPTER X.

Catholic missionaries—Methods of the priests—Wholesale baptisms—Indians not permanently benefited—Proofs of failure—Their missions reinforced—Complaints of Dr. Whitman—His great generosity—Events prior to the massacre—Indians influenced by priests and others—Destruction of Protestant mission the result.. 120

CHAPTER XI.

The controversy over the massacre continued—Defense made by accused parties—Indians hostile to Dr. Whitman had resolved to kill him—Reasons assigned—Charges of taking their lands and poisoning them—Deaths by disease—Accounts of the massacre by priests and Hudson Bay Company—Causes stated inadequate—Some of the statements false—Approximate causes... 135

CHAPTER XII.

The murderers Cayuse Indians—Roman Catholic half-breeds and Hudson Bay employés the instigators—Object to break up the Protestant missions—Catholics and Hudson Bay people unharmed—Active agency of half-breeds—Indirect influence of priests over Indians—They and Hudson Bay Company blamed—Conclusions from the evidence................. 152

CHAPTER XIII.

Survivors at Waiilatpu—Proper sympathy and aid not extended to them—Hudson Bay Company blamed for not preventing the massacre—Its agents charged with cruelty to Messrs. Hall and Osborne—Miss Bewley's sufferings—Her deposition—Lack of protection at the priests' camp................... 169

CHAPTER XIV.

Dr. Whitman's journey East in 1842-43—Its purpose—Visit to Washington and influence there both questioned—Confirmed by his letters, and by a Congressional bill—His patriotic and valuable services—Evidence that he more than any other person, saved Oregon to the United States.............. 183

APPENDIX.

Letter from Dr. Whitman to James M. Porter, Secretary of War.. 197
Whitman's Ride.. 205

THE STORY OF MARCUS WHITMAN.

CHAPTER I.

OREGON.—THE CONTEST FOR POSSESSION.

ORIGINALLY, the territory of Oregon comprised all the country lying between the Rocky Mountains and the Pacific Ocean, bounded on the north by the Russian possessions, latitude 54° 40′, and on the south by the northern border of California, latitude 42°. It extended seven hundred and fifty miles from north to south, and about five hundred miles from east to west, being nearly four times the size of Great Britain and Ireland combined. This huge territory was claimed, wholly or in part, by five powers—Spain, France, Russia, Great Britain and the United States.

By the law of nations, the title to any country depends upon the first discovery and occupancy of it, or upon purchase or cession by treaty from the first discoverer or occupant. "When a nation takes possession of a country to which no prior owner can lay claim," says Vattel, "it is considered as acquiring the empire or sovereignty of it. When a nation finds a country uninhabited and without an owner, it may lawfully take possession of it; and after it has sufficiently made known its will in this respect, it cannot be deprived of it by any other nation."

It is almost universally conceded that Spanish navigators were the first discoverers and first explorers of the northwest coast of America. After their conquests in Mexico they explored the adjacent seas and countries, and in 1543 discovered California. Nine years afterward they extended their exploration of the coast to Cape Blanco, 43° north latitude; in 1582 to 57° 40′, and in 1588 to Bering Strait. In 1592 Juan de Fuca discovered and entered the straits which bear his name, but for nearly two centuries thereafter the Spanish career of discovery was substantially at a standstill. In 1774–75 the Viceroy of Mexico fitted out two expeditions which surveyed the coast from Monterey up to latitude 54°, discovering Nootka Sound, the Island of Vancouver and the mouth of the Columbia River. Spanish vessels from Mexico in 1792 also surveyed many of the bays and channels which lie between the 52d and 56th parallels.

The rights of Spain, founded on discovery, were recognized, after a vigorous dispute, in the Nootka Convention of 1790, in which she yielded the right to navigate, trade and fish on the northwest coast, but reserved her sovereignty over the entire territory described in the opening paragraph of this chapter. This treaty was reaffirmed in 1814, when Great Britain assented anew to Spain's territorial claims. The rights of Spain were transferred in turn to the United States by the Florida treaty of 1819, wherein "His Catholic Majesty cedes all his rights, claims and pretensions to any territories north of the 42d parallel of latitude." The boundary line thus defined was confirmed in 1828 by Mexico, which had obtained its independence. Meanwhile, France having acquired possession of Louisiana by cession from Spain in 1800, the United States, in 1803, purchased "all its rights and appurtenances, as fully and in the same manner as it had been acquired from Spain;" and the northern boundary of Louisiana had been declared in 1763, by the treaty of Versailles between Great Britain and France, "to be a line drawn due west from the source of the Mississippi, assigning to England the territory north of the 49th parallel of latitude and east of the Mississippi."

Russia having asserted her right to all the northwest coast and the islands north of latitude 51°, and Great Britain and the United States having protested, a protracted correspondence had taken place, ending in an agreement, in 1824, that Russia should make no claim south of 54° 40', or the United States north of the same line. This left but two contestants for possession of Oregon—Great Britain and the United States.

The claims of the United States did not rest solely on the rights transferred to them by treaty from other powers; they claimed sovereignty by right of discovery as well. In 1787 Captains Gray and Kendrick sailed from Boston for the northwest coast, and in September of the following year reached Nootka, where they passed the winter. In 1791 Captain Gray surveyed the Straits of Fuca, whence he sailed to Canton and thence to the United States. He made a second voyage to the Pacific, and on the 11th of May, 1792, discovered the mouth of the Columbia River, which he ascended twenty miles, trading with the natives and examining the country. In the meantime Captain Kendrick, who had remained on the coast, purchased from the native chiefs several large tracts of land near Nootka Sound, for the use of the commercial company he represented. From 1791 onward the northwest coast was visited yearly by many vessels from the United States engaged in trading enterprises, each expedition making new discoveries or adding to the knowledge of the territory already discovered; and from 1766 to about 1815 the direct trade between the northwest coast and Canton was carried on exclusively by American vessels sailing under our own flag.

Great Britain claimed priority of discovery of the Columbia River by Lieutenant Mears in 1788 and by Vancouver in 1792. But Mears' vessel was fitted out at Macoa, a Portuguese port, bore sailing papers written in the Portuguese language and sailed under the Portuguese flag; and both his journal and Vancouver's show that they not only did not discover the Columbia, but that they actually affirmed the impossibility of its existence from the nature of the coast, in spite of the fact that Captain Gray had informed Vancouver of his discovery when they met, the April before, in the Straits of Fuca. This seems to dispose of Great Britain's claims based on prior discovery of the Columbia River.

By way of perfecting their rights the United States began, within a reasonable time, as required by the law of nations, to examine the territory with a view to forming settlements. President Jefferson, with the approval of Congress, commissioned Captains Lewis and Clark* in

* In the Report of the expedition it is printed Clarke. Captain Clark wrote his name without the final vowel, as may be seen from his official

1804, and instructed them to proceed to Oregon and explore the Columbia River from its source to the Pacific Ocean. This they did, taking possession of the country as a part of the United States and making an encampment which they named Fort Clatsop, where they passed the winter of 1805-6.

In 1808 the Missouri Fur Company established a trading post on the head waters of Lewis River, one of the principal branches of the Columbia; and the Pacific Fur Company, with John Jacob Astor at its head, sent out the ship *Tonquin* in 1810, with the necessary persons and material to establish posts for carrying on an active trade with the natives, in furs and other commodities. Arriving at the mouth of the Columbia in March, 1811, the party selected a site for the principal factory, eight miles from the ocean, and named it Astoria. These were the first permanent settlements made in the territory of Oregon and the first steps taken to hold and civilize the country. They constitute the third claim, and a very strong one, in behalf of the United States.

Nevertheless, Great Britain continued her contest. Many vain attempts to reconcile the conflicting interests of the two countries by negotiation served to increase rather than allay existing jealousies and animosities, and war at one time appeared almost unavoidable. The peace policy, however, finally prevailed, and the right of ownership was settled in June, 1846, by a treaty concluded in the city of Washington. By its terms the boundary line

---

correspondence with the Government while Superintendent of Indian Affairs in the Northwest. Hereafter his name will appear as he spelled it in this book.

between the territorial possessions of the two countries was to begin at "the point on the forty-ninth parallel of north latitude, where the boundary laid down in existing treaties and conventions* between the United States and Great Britain terminates, and shall continue westward along the said forty-ninth parallel of north latitude to the middle of the channel which separates the continent from Vancouver's Island, and thence southerly through the middle of the said channel and of Fuca's Straits to the Pacific Ocean." There were two conditions connected with this: First, that the navigation of said channel and straits south of the forty-ninth parallel was to be open and free to both parties; and, second, that all possessory rights acquired by British subjects were to be respected.

One indefinite element in the treaty of 1846 afterward caused great trouble. As it was impossible accurately to define the water part of the boundary line, this was left to be subsequently settled by a Commission. This Commission never reached any satisfactory conclusion, owing to the diverse interpretations given to the first article of the treaty. Nor were later efforts for the settlement of this vexed question by the statesmen of Great Britain and the United States more successful. Great Britain insisted that by "the middle of the channel" was meant the waters of the Straits of Rosario; while the United States asserted just as positively that it meant the Canal de Haro, the most direct and best route to the Pacific Ocean. Great Britain claimed that the boundary line should run east of

---

* The allusion to existing conventions and treaties refers to those of 1818 and 1827, and especially to the Ashburton treaty in 1842, by which the boundary line east of the Rocky Mountains was established, from the Bay of Fundy to the Lake of the Woods.

the Island of San Juan; the United States, that it should run west of the island, and between it and Vancouver's Island, thus leaving San Juan in possession of the United States.

Thus the controversy continued between the two countries until the treaty of Washington, in May, 1871, provided for submitting the question at issue "to the arbitration and award of His Majesty the Emperor of Germany," whose decision should be final and without appeal, both parties agreeing to give effect to it "without any objection, evasion, or delay whatsoever." The case of the United States was submitted in December, 1871, by Hon. George Bancroft, our Minister at Berlin; and the case of Great Britain by Admiral Prevost. The award was made in October, 1872, the Emperor decreeing "that the claim of the United States of America is most in accordance with the true interpretation of the treaty of 1846." The promptness and good faith with which the British Government gave effect to this decision brought to a friendly close the last of a series of boundary controversies which had been waged between two of the most important nations of the world for not less than ninety years.

CHAPTER II.

EXPLORATION BY ORDER OF CONGRESS.

IN 1803, the same year in which Louisiana was purchased from France, and before the transfer of the territory was completed, President Jefferson addressed a confidential message to Congress recommending that measures be taken without delay for the examination of the country west of the Rocky Mountains. Congress approving, Captains Merriweather Lewis and William Clark were commissioned to have charge of the expedition. They were instructed to explore the Missouri River to its source, and then to seek for some stream running to the Pacific, "whether the Columbia, the Oregon, the Colorado, or any other which might offer the most direct and practicable water communication across the continent, for the purposes of commerce; and to trace the same to its termination in the Pacific."

The party under command of Captain Lewis, consisting of thirty men, set out for the West, expecting to advance some distance up the Missouri River before ice should prevent further progress. They were not permitted, however, to pass beyond the Mississippi, the Spanish commander of this territory not having been informed of its transfer to the United States. Consequently it was not until May, 1804, that they began the ascent of the Missouri. The current was so strong that their three boats made but slow progress, and October had passed before they arrived in the country of the Mandan Indians, some 1600 miles from the mouth of the river, where they went into camp.

Resuming their voyage up the Missouri on the 7th of April, 1805, in three weeks they reached the junction of the Yellowstone. Soon afterward their progress was arrested by what was then known as the Great Falls of the Missouri, and nearly a month was consumed in transporting the canoes and their cargoes to a point above the falls, and in constructing additional boats out of the large trees that grew on the river banks. In July they went on, and passed through the gates of the Rocky Mountains, a narrow channel six miles long, where the river breaks through the mountains. Above here a large number of streams flow into the Missouri; the largest of these, which they named the Jefferson, they explored to its source near the forty-fourth degree of latitude, about 3000 miles from where they began the ascent of the Missouri. Abandoning their canoes, and storing a portion of their goods at the head of the Jefferson River, the party provided themselves with horses and guides from the Shoshone Indians, and on the 30th of August began their journey through the Rocky Mountains.

This was by far the most difficult part of their route. They underwent, says Capt. Clark, "every suffering which hunger, cold and fatigue could impose." Food was insufficient, and difficult to procure, consisting of berries, dried fish, and the meat of dogs and horses; the mountains were high, and the passes were rough and frequently covered with snow. They crossed many streams flowing westward; finally, on the 7th of October, they embarked on one of the largest of these, in five canoes which they had constructed, and descended it till they reached a river, which they named the Lewis, and which proved to be the principal southern tributary of the Columbia. Continuing their voyage on the Lewis for seven days more, they came to its confluence with the larger northern branch, to which they gave the name Clark. Passing down the Columbia, whose waters they had now reached, they arrived at the great falls on the 22d of October, and on the 30th, at the lower falls, a short distance below which they saw the tides of the Pacific. On the 17th of November the horizon line of the ocean was visible, and all realized that the exploration was complete, and that a new way had been discovered through the trackless wilderness between the Eastern States and the Northwest coast.

A landing was made on the north bank of the river, but the party afterwards crossed to the south side, where they formed an encampment, giving it the name of Fort Clatsop. Here the winter of 1805–6 was passed; but the rains were so frequent, long continued and violent that comparatively little could be done in the way of surveys or explorations of the river and adjacent country.

The explorers began their return voyage to the United States on the 23d of March, 1806. Before leaving, they prepared an account of their outward journey, which was written on parchment and posted in the fort, copies being given also to the natives for the benefit of any who might come after. It stated that the expedition had been sent out by the United States Government, and had reached the Pacific Ocean through the Rocky Mountains, and by way of the Missouri and Columbia Rivers.

Ascending the Columbia in canoes, the party reached the falls, about 125 miles from the Pacific, by the middle of April. On their way up they discovered a large stream flowing into the Columbia from the north, called the Cowlitz by the natives, and another, the Willamette, thirty miles away, joining the Columbia on the south. From the falls the exploring party proceeded by land to the Rocky Mountains, and through them to the Clark River, where it was agreed that the chiefs of the expedition should separate, to meet again at the junction of the Yellowstone and Missouri Rivers.

The party under Captain Lewis first proceeded down the Clark River, then crossed the mountains to the headwaters of the Maria River, which they followed down to its union with the Missouri. Captain Clark and his party journeyed southward, up the valley of the Clark to the sources of that stream, then crossed the mountains to the head-waters of the Yellowstone, which they descended in canoes to the Missouri, meeting Lewis and his men on the 12th of August. The united party embarked on the Missouri, and reached St. Louis on the 23d of September, 1806, having traveled, in going and returning, more than 9000 miles.

This expedition was a great success, judged by the extent and value of the discoveries made, though it was not the first passage of the Rocky Mountains by whites. Alexander Mackenzie had crossed them in 1789, and again in 1792; in his first journey reaching the Arctic Ocean, and in his second the tide-waters of the Pacific at Vancouver. French and Spanish fur traders, also, had previously ascended the Missouri as far as the mouth of the Yellowstone; but comparatively little correct knowledge of the river or the adjacent country was possessed before the Lewis and Clark explorations. The journals of the latter furnished the first authentic and definite accounts we have of that vast territory between the falls of the Missouri and those of the Columbia; they were long regarded as the principal source of information respecting the geography, the natural history, and the aboriginal inhabitants of that part of the continent.

It was, therefore, only three or four years after this great territory came into our possession that its principal features were made known, and the Government of the United States evinced its intention to occupy and settle the country.

CHAPTER III.

AMERICAN SETTLEMENTS.

THE success of the expedition of Lewis and Clark arrested public attention, and speedily led to the organization of a number of companies for engaging in the fur trade with the natives of the Northwest. The first of these, the Missouri Fur Company, was formed in 1808, in St. Louis, and during the next two years established trading posts on the upper Mississippi and Missouri Rivers, and one west of the Rocky Mountains on Lewis River, the great southern branch of the Columbia. The latter was undoubtedly the first permanent establishment in the country drained by the Columbia and its tributaries. It was abandoned in 1810 on account of the difficulty of securing provisions, but more particularly because of the hostility of the Indians in the vicinity.

The first attempt to form a permanent settlement on the Columbia River itself was made in the early part of 1809, by some Bostonians, prominent among them the three brothers Winship. The ship *Albatross* was placed under command of Nathan Winship, and fitted out not only with everything necessary for trade with the natives, but also with materials for building, and for cultivation of the soil. The vessel reached the mouth of the Columbia in May, 1810, and ascended the river to a place called Oak

Point, where a house was built, land cleared and a garden planted. The site selected proved unfortunate in many respects, and was abandoned the same year.

John Jacob Astor, of New York City, organized in 1810 the Pacific Fur Company, for the prosecution of the fur trade in the northwestern parts of the continent, in connection with commerce with China. The inception of the scheme was wholly Mr. Astor's, and he furnished the money necessary for its execution. His plan was to establish posts on the Missouri and Columbia Rivers, and on the coast contiguous to the latter, where the furs were to be collected for shipment either east to the United States, or to China where they could be exchanged for silks and tea. These posts were to be furnished with provisions and articles for barter with the Indians, either by way of the Missouri River, or by vessels direct from New York City. The principal post or factory, Astoria, was located near the mouth of the Columbia, and was to be the depot of supplies for all the others, and the general depository for the furs purchased. It was also the purpose of the Company to engage largely in trade with the Russian settlements on the Pacific, receiving furs in payment for provisions and other articles.

This was a wise and comprehensive plan, and, at the time it was undertaken, appeared entirely practicable. For its more successful prosecution, Mr. Astor admitted as partners, Wilson G. Hunt, John Clarke and Robert McClellan, citizens of the United States; and Alexander McKay, Duncan McDougall, Donald McKenzie, David and Robert Stuart, and Ramsey Crooks, Canadians. The voyageurs were nearly all Canadians, with Alexander McKay as commander; while the majority of the clerks were Americans, and Mr. Hunt was made chief agent on the Pacific coast. The stock was divided into one hundred shares, half of which was owned by the projector; the remainder was divided equally among his partners. Mr. Astor agreed to furnish goods to the value of $400,000, bear all losses for five years and divide the profits if any.

The first expedition, consisting of four of the Scotch or Canadian partners, with eleven clerks and thirteen Canadian voyageurs, sailed from New York in September, 1810, on the ship *Tonquin*. In January, 1811, the second party left St. Louis, in charge of Mr. Hunt, accompanied by Messrs. McKenzie, McClellan and Crooks; and in October, the ship *Beaver* carried out from New York Mr. Clarke and several additional clerks.

The *Tonquin* arrived at the mouth of the Columbia in March, 1811, and the passengers were landed on the shore of Baker's Bay. From this they removed to a high point of land on the south bank of the river ten miles from the ocean, where preparations were begun at once for building a fort and the other buildings necessary for the safety of the occupants, and for an extensive and lucrative trade with the natives. Astoria was the name given to the fort, in honor of the originator of the company. The ship which had borne them to the coast, after landing its passengers and freight, sailed north to collect furs from the Russians, and to make additional arrangements for future trading.

While building the fort, the Americans received a visit from a party of men belonging to the North West Company, under the leadership of a Mr. Thompson, who had been sent from Canada the previous year with instructions to occupy the mouth of the river before the Americans should effect a settlement there. On their way down the Columbia, the party had built huts and named the more prominent points on the river, thus taking formal possession, as they supposed, of all the territory; but having been detained on their journey and compelled to winter in the Rocky Mountains, they arrived too late to accomplish their purpose. The British Government, through its commissioners, afterward claimed that Thompson's occupation of the country was prior to that of the Pacific Fur Company. As a matter of fact, however, Captains Lewis and Clark descended the Columbia to its mouth in November, 1805; while the North West Company established their first post beyond the Rocky Mountains in 1806, and this was far north of any part of the Columbia River.

When Mr. Thompson and his company returned northward, they were accompanied by a party from the American fort under charge of David Stuart, who established a trading post at the confluence of the Okanagon River with the Columbia, four hundred miles above Astoria. Several other posts were built during this and the following year by the Astor Company. The principal one was on the Spokan; it was used as a place of trade up to 1825, being occupied afterward successively by the North West Company and the Hudson Bay Company.

The party of sixty men under the Chief Agent, Mr. Hunt, who were to ascend the Missouri River and cross the Rocky Mountains to the head-waters of the Columbia, reached Astoria by way of the latter river in the spring of 1812. They suffered much from hunger and cold, the opposition of rival companies, and the hostility of the Indians. Scarcely had they reached their destination when word was brought by the natives of the destruction of the ship *Tonquin* and the massacre of the entire crew by the Indians near the Straits of Fuca.

In May, 1812, the ship *Beaver* arrived at the factory, bringing the third detachment of persons in the service of the Company, and a large amount of supplies. Notwithstanding the severe blow occasioned by the loss of the *Tonquin*, the surviving partners determined to prosecute the enterprise with increasing energy; and Mr. Hunt was dispatched in the *Beaver* to complete the commercial arrangements with the Russian settlements on the northern coasts, leaving Mr. McDougall in charge of the fort.

The affairs of the Company were at this time prosperous; provisions were abundant, and a large quantity of furs had been collected, awaiting the return of the *Beaver* to transport them to China; when in January, 1813, news reached Astoria that war had begun between the United States and Great Britain. This was followed by information that the *Beaver* was blockaded by a British cruiser in the port of Canton, whither it had gone with a cargo of furs instead of returning to the Columbia.

Two agents of the North West Company named McTavish and Laroque arrived at Astoria soon afterward, bringing reports of British victories on the northern frontier of the United States, and of a British naval expedition on its way to take possession of the Columbia River. They were received by Mr. McDougall and Mr. McKenzie, the only partners of the Pacific Fur Company at the factory, with every mark of friendship, and supplied with provisions from the stores of the fort; and also, as some authorities state, with goods for trading with the Indians. They were treated, in short, as if they had been allies and not rivals and foes. The exigencies of the situation led to secret conferences between hosts and guests, resulting finally in the announcement by Messrs. McDougall and McKenzie that they would dissolve the Pacific Fur Company on the 1st of the following June, should no relief come meanwhile. They made known their decision to the other resident partners, Messrs. Stuart and Clarke, who were absent at the Company's two principal neighbor posts; but both these men opposed the idea of abandoning the property of the Company, and, on the ground that assistance might still reach them from the United States, secured the promise of a few months' delay. In the meantime several of the employés at Astoria left and went into the service of the North West Company.

The hoped-for relief came not. Mr. Astor had sent out the ship *Lark* in March, 1813, with men and supplies, but unfortunately it was wrecked near one of the Hawaiian Islands. The frigate *Adams* was ordered by the United States Government to the North Pacific to protect the establishment at Astoria; but just as she was ready to sail from New York it became necessary to transfer her crew to Lake Ontario to repel the British in that direction, and the blockade of American ports by the enemy prevented all further efforts at protection.

During this interval the North West Company's party had returned to Astoria and stated that an armed ship was on its way from London for the purpose of destroying everything American which might be found on the Northwest coast. They accordingly renewed their offer to purchase at a fair valuation all the buildings, furs and stock in hand of the Pacific Fur Company. The terms of sale were accepted, after much bargaining and delay, by McDougall, who was in charge of the factory; and on the 16th of October, 1813, the contract of sale was signed, by which the price to be paid was set at $40,000.*

Scarcely had the sale been completed and the movable property transferred from the factory to the boats of the North West Company, when a British sloop-of-war entered the Columbia, hoping to secure a rich prize in the capture of Astoria with its supply of provisions and its collection of furs. The United States flag was still on the factory, and McDougall in charge ready to surrender on demand; but all that could make the capture valuable was already far up the Columbia, on board the barges of the rival company. Nothing was left to the British captain but the satisfaction of lowering the American and hoisting the English flag and renaming the factory, Fort George.

Mr. Hunt, the general agent of the Pacific Fur Company, learning that a British force had been ordered to the Pacific for the purpose of seizing the American possessions on the Columbia, proceeded at once to the Hawaiian Islands and chartered the American brig *Pedlar*, in which he

---

* Bancroft, "$80,000."

Wheeler says, "about $58,000;" but this is of slight importance. Mr. Gray states that the appraised value of the furs alone at the factory was $36,835.50, leaving but little more than $3000 for all the buildings at Astoria, and those at Okanagon and Spokan, which, with the necessary equipments for trade, had cost the company nearly $200,000. When it became necessary for the United States to purchase this property in 1865, the Hudson Bay Company, after using it for more than forty years, asked for the three establishments more than $100,000.

sailed for Astoria, where he arrived in February, 1814. But he found the sale consummated, the property removed, and McDougall superintending the factory as agent and partner of the North West Company. Mr. Hunt could do nothing but receive the Montreal bills given in payment for the Company's effects; with these he reëmbarked in the *Pedlar*, and proceeded to the United States by way of Canton.

Such was the inglorious ending of Mr. Astor's well-planned scheme to establish settlements and trade on the Pacific coast. Its failure was due to no lack of wisdom in its inception or of resources for its successful prosecution, but chiefly to circumstances which could not reasonably have been anticipated. One of these was the war with Great Britain, which made all communication with the settlements, either by sea or land, uncertain and difficult, and rendered the furs collected of little value as they could not be transported by the Company's vessels to a market in China; another was the treachery of Mr. Astor's Canadian partners, who, during Mr. Hunt's absence from Astoria, entered into a compact with agents of the North West Company for the sale of the property that had been left in their custody. It is not surprising that Mr. Astor declared, when he heard of the transaction, that he would have much preferred the capture and destruction of all his property by the enemy, to seeing it bartered away in so disgraceful a manner.

We are aware that Mr. Greenhow, in his history of Oregon, presents a plausible excuse for the conduct of the agents who effected the sale, although admitting that their motives will ever be open to suspicion. Not being citizens of the United States, he reasons, they could not be expected to resist with force an attempt to seize the forts and property of the Company; and believing these to be in danger of capture, they resorted to a sale as the best method of protecting the interests of all concerned.

Other writers have adopted this view, or have been content to ascribe the war of 1812 as a sufficient cause for the failure of the Astor enterprise. Rev. Myron Eells, for instance, in his *History of Indian Missions on the Pacific Coast*,* states that "Astoria was sold to the Northwestern Fur Company owing to the war of 1812 with England."

As opposed to this, and confirmatory of the view given above, we have the statement of Gabriel Franchere, a British subject from Montreal who was connected with the Pacific Fur Company, and was at Astoria when all the transactions took place. In his volume entitled *Northwest Coast of America*, p. 178, he says: "Mr. Hunt (who had returned from the Sandwich Islands) was surprised beyond measure when we informed him of the resolution we had taken of abandoning the country; he blamed us severely for having acted with so much precipitation." On p. 191 he gives an account of the "stratagem" of the North West Company to get possession, by representing through a letter of Mr. Shaw, a partner of that company, that the ship *Isaac Todd* and the frigate *Phœbe* had sailed from England with orders from the Government to seize the establishment. He further states that this had a most important influence in selling; and complains of "such treatment on the part of the British Government, after the assurance we had received from Mr. Jackson, His Majesty's

* P. 151.

Chargé d'affaires, previous to our departure from New York." And then, on p. 203, he shows how easily the property of the Pacific Fur Company could have been saved from capture by the British sloop-of-war. " It was only necessary to get rid of the land party of the North West Company, who were completely in our power, then remove our effects by boat up the river upon some small stream, and await the result."

This is precisely what was done with the property by the North West Company, after getting possession of it.* "The charge of treason to Mr. Astor's interests, in the eyes of the world, will always be attached to their characters, McDougall and McKenzie, Astor's partners. McDougall, as a reward for betraying the trust reposed in him, was made a partner in the North West Company."

Mrs. Victor passes the same judgment upon the transaction. "The Canadian partners," she says, "took advantage of the situation to betray Mr. Astor's interests."†

---

* Hubert Bancroft says that the property could not have been thus saved by the members of the Company, as the Indians and the North West Company would have prevented their getting supplies—that the latter Company was determined to drive them out.

† *River of the West*, p. 34.

CHAPTER IV.

FOREIGN TRADING COMPANIES.

OF the foreign companies, claiming exclusive privileges of trade in this vast country, the North West, though not the first formed, was the first to come into active competition with American enterprises; and, as we have seen, succeeded to the property at Astoria and to the trade so auspiciously begun there. The Company was organized in 1784,* at Montreal, and its forty shares were distributed among the men engaged directly in its service, in this way securing their devotion to its interests. Part of the stock was held by the agents, who resided in Montreal and supplied goods and the necessary capital; the rest by the partners, who conducted the business at the interior trading posts or forts, and the clerks, who traded directly with the natives. Goods required for the trade were imported from England, and then carried in boats to the most distant posts of the Company; and the furs obtained in exchange were sent back in the same way to Montreal.

Desiring to extend its trade as rapidly as possible, the Company sent out several exploring expeditions. The first, led by Mackenzie, in 1789, discovered the Mackenzie River and followed it to the ocean. The second, in 1793,

* Bancroft, 1793.

under the same intrepid explorer, started from Fort Chipewan and crossed the American continent at its widest part, and, by way of Frazer's River, reached the Pacific Ocean at the mouth of an inlet named by Vancouver the Cascade Canal. Other agents of the Company explored the country southwest to the foot of the Rocky Mountains, the region drained by the head-waters of the Missouri. In this way a more accurate knowledge was obtained of the country, while avenues were opened for a prosperous and greatly extended trade. Its explorations west of the Rocky Mountains, however, were all far north of the waters of the Columbia River.

The first establishment founded by the North West Company west of the Rocky Mountains was in 1805, on McLeod Lake, near the 54th parallel of latitude; its purpose was to give the Company eventual control of the trade in the entire country watered by the Columbia and its tributaries. Such efforts were natural and to be expected, as the expedition of Lewis and Clark excited the jealousy of the British Government and all the foreign trading companies, and led the North West Company to send a party in all haste down the northern branch of the Columbia in 1811 to secure prior possession. It continued to be the settled policy of this Company to drive out of the country all parties engaged in trade with the Indians, so that it might maintain its monopoly in furs. Nor was it scrupulous as to means. If fair competition would not avail it did not hesitate to resort to the most unjustifiable measures, even to exciting the natives to plunder and murder.

But while thus actively engaged in extending its trade

across the continent and supplanting the enterprise and influence of others, and especially all American traders, it encountered a formidable competitor and rival in the Hudson Bay Company, which could not be subdued and driven from the field.

This Company owed its origin to a charter granted in 1670 by Charles II to an association of London merchants, covering all the region of country surrounding Hudson Bay. An important consideration in granting the charter was that, through the explorations of agents of the association, the regions lying west of Hudson and Baffin Bays would be made known and a means of water communication discovered between the Atlantic and Pacific Oceans. The management of the Company was placed in the hands of a governor or deputy governor and a committee of seven members residing in London, and the powers conferred were exclusive and well-nigh sovereign. The charter gave the grantees not only the entire trade and commerce of that vast region, but also made them proprietors of the territory, and authorized them to establish courts and enact civil and criminal laws for the government of their possessions. All other persons were forbidden, under heavy penalties, to trade within their domain, and they were empowered to build fortifications to protect their rights and property against intruders throughout that portion of America drained by streams entering Hudson Bay.

Under such encouraging conditions this powerful corporation gradually extended its influence among the natives and established its trading posts, till in due course it set about the destruction of all troublesome rivals, including the North West Company. The plan adopted was to grant to Lord Selkirk, a Scotch nobleman, 100,000 square miles of land around Red River for purposes of colonization. To have this territory thus occupied would have been ruinous to the North West Company, whose chief route from Canada to their northwestern trading posts ran through it, while from it were obtained most of the provisions required for those posts. The validity of the grant was therefore denied by the North West Company and resistance made to the settlement of the country; and when finally the governor of the new province attempted by proclamation to prohibit all persons from trading within its limits, a deadly feud began between the two great corporations. In 1816 their respective adherents engaged in a bloody battle near Fort Douglas, in which the Hudson Bay party were defeated and twenty-two of them killed, including the governor, and the fort occupied by the victors.

This only served to intensify the hostility between the companies, who, enlisting their employés and the Indians over whom they had influence, engaged in frequent and bloody strifes, until they wiped out well-nigh the entire profits of the fur trade and endangered the lives of all white men by the savage feelings they had excited among the natives.

This condition of affairs was brought before the British Parliament in 1810 and a compromise was effected, whereby the rival corporations were united in July, 1821, under the name of the Hudson Bay Company. The united Company received grants for exclusive trade for twenty-one years in all the territory north of Canada and the

United States and in that west of the Rocky Mountains; and the servants of the Company were commissioned to act as justices of peace, so that the jurisdiction of the courts of Upper Canada was carried to the shores of the Pacific.

This union proved most advantageous, and the Hudson Bay Company spared neither effort nor expense to acquire influence over all the Indian tribes and to erect trading posts west of the Rocky Mountains, especially on the Columbia River and its tributaries. "The agents of the Company," says Mr. Greenhow, "were seen in every part of the continent, north and northwest of the United States and Canada, from the Atlantic to the Pacific, hunting, trapping and trading with the aborigines; its boats went on every stream and lake, conveying British goods into the interior or furs to the great depositories on each ocean, for shipment to England in British vessels. Of the trading posts, many were fortified and could be defended by their inmates—men inured to hardships and dangers—against all attacks which might be apprehended; and the whole vast expanse of territory, including the regions drained by the Columbia, was, in fact, occupied by British forces and governed by British laws, though there was not a single British soldier, technically speaking, within its limits."

The Company succeeded so well and became so powerful that American citizens were obliged not only to relinquish all hope of trade in the interior but even to withdraw their vessels from the coast. It had in the year 1846, according to the testimony of Sir James Douglas, 55 officers and 513 articled men in its employ. These were all bound by a strict agreement to subserve, under all circumstances, the interests of the Company, and were forbidden to acquire any personal or real estate, were dependent upon their pay as its servants, and were subject to any punishment which should be inflicted by the officer in charge for neglect of duty. It had twenty-three forts and five trading stations judiciously situated for its business and forming a network of posts supporting each other. It had trading parties extending into California, Utah, Arizona, Montana and the Rocky Mountains, and north along the northwestern water-shed of the Rocky Mountains. It had two steamers to enter all the bays, harbors and rivers of the Pacific coast from Mexico to Russian America. With this number of men and resources we can readily admit Sir James Douglas' claim that the Company "possessed an extraordinary influence with the Indians, and in 1846 practically enjoyed a monopoly of the fur trade in the country west of the Rocky Mountains."

Similar testimony as to the Company's power is given in a report of the Senate Committee on Foreign Affairs in 1839, by Mr. Hall J. Kelley, who visited Oregon in 1835 and 1836. "The Company exercise full authority over all," he says, "whether Indians, English or Americans, who are in its service, and in a manner always injurious and generally disastrous to all others who undertake to trade or settle in the territory. It may be said, in fact, that Americans, except associated with this Company, are not permitted to carry on a traffic within several hundred miles of the Company's posts." He proceeds to show how the trade and commerce of the coast, as well as the inland trade, had been cut off. Whenever a vessel appeared the Company despatched one of its own, with orders to follow her from port to port, undersell her, and drive her off the coast at any sacrifice. Mr. Simpson, who had charge of this part of the Company's business, declared that it was "resolved, even at the cost of a hundred thousand pounds, to expel the Americans from traffic on that coast."

Mr. J. K. Townsend, a naturalist who visited Oregon in 1834, wholly in the interests of his favorite science, and who remained there two years, after speaking of the many acts of kindness he had received from the agents of the Hudson Bay Company, says: "Travelers, and all who are not traders, are kindly treated; but the moment the visitor is known to trade a beaver skin from an Indian, that moment he is ejected from the community, and all communication between him and the officers of the Company ceases. When Captain Wyeth* with his party arrived at Walla Walla Fort, on his passage down the Columbia, he was required by the superintendent to promise that during his journey from thence to Vancouver—300 miles—he would not buy a beaver skin; the functionary assuring him that unless he consented so to bind himself, he would send a party ahead of him to purchase every beaver skin at a price which he could not afford to pay." He further states that the Company had a large sum of money which it employed solely for the purpose "of opposing all who may come to interfere with their monopoly, by purchasing, at exorbitant prices, all the furs in the possession of the Indians, and thus forcing the settler to come to terms, or driving him from the country."

* Mr. Townsend entered Oregon in company with Captain Wyeth.

The evidence of Mr. Greenhow on this point is valuable as coming from the friendliest source. We can readily admit what he says about the kindness and hospitality shown by the Company to strangers in that country, so long as they did not in the remotest manner interfere with its commercial monopoly; but even he admits that when "any one unconnected with the Company attempted to hunt, or trap, or trade with the natives, then all the force of the body was immediately turned toward him."

Mr. Greenhow asserts also that the Company endeavored "to prevent the vessels of the United States from obtaining cargoes on the northwest coasts;" and that "the publications made by the directors and agents of the Hudson Bay Company evince the most hostile feelings toward the citizens of the United States, against whom every species of calumny is leveled in those works."

A further method employed by the Company for retaining control of all the trade of the country was to place arbitrary and unjust restrictions on all commerce with the Indians. It fixed the prices to be paid for furs according to its own low and mercenary standard, and any deviation from this tariff was sure to incur the displeasure of the monopoly. Nor was this exacted alone of its own agents and employés. Its power was such that no person dared to oppose its arbitrary commands, as implicit obedience was the condition of its favor and protection. The policy thus pursued for purposes of trade would necessarily be antagonistic to permanent settlement of the country and rapid increase of the population. The Indians must be discouraged in all their attempts to adopt civilized methods of life, as they would then abandon the pursuit of fur-bearing animals; and the entire country must be preserved in its wild, primitive condition, to furnish a suitable home for the fox, the bear, and the beaver. Sir Edward Fitzgerald thus summed it up: "The Hudson Bay Company has entailed misery and destruction upon thousands throughout the country which is withering under its curse. . . . . It has stopped the extension of civilization, and has excluded the light of religious truth." It was a despotic government, he declared, which had so used its monopoly of commerce and its power, "as to shut up the earth from the knowledge of man, and man from the knowledge of God."

In its desire to discourage immigration from every quarter, but more especially from the United States, the Company adopted two measures. The first was to represent the land as sterile, and not susceptible of profitable cultivation — "an unbroken waste of sand deserts and impassable mountains, fit only for the beaver, the gray bear and the savage." The second was to discourage all immigration from the East, by representing that insurmountable obstacles were in the way—mountains and rivers that could not be crossed; deserts where famine would surely ensue; distances so great that the snows of a polar winter would overwhelm the immigrant before he could reach any settlement; and hostile savages ever ready to plunder and murder the defenseless traveler. These representations deterred most persons from attempts to penetrate the then unknown region; a few who were more resolute and venturesome, and who set out upon the long journey, were turned back by the agents of the Company at its eastern forts.

General Palmer says in his journal (p. 43): "While we

remained at this place (Fort Hall), great efforts were made to induce the immigrants to pursue the route to California. The most extravagant tales were related respecting the dangers awaiting a trip to Oregon, and the difficulties and trials to be surmounted. . . . . For instance, the crossings of Snake River, and the crossings of the Columbia and other smaller streams, were represented as being attended with great danger. . . . . In addition to the above, it was asserted that three or four tribes of Indians in the middle regions had combined for the purpose of preventing our passage through their country. In case we escaped destruction at the hands of the savages, that a more fearful enemy—famine—would attend our march, as the distance was so great that winter would overtake us before making the Cascade mountains."

Were it necessary to multiply evidence, statements could be produced from the Company's own agents, showing its fixed purpose to exclude American settlers. At this time, 1832, let it be borne in mind that the Company exercised exclusive civil and commercial jurisdiction from the Russian settlement on the north to the Gulf of California on the south and from the Rocky Mountains on the east to the Pacific Ocean on the west, leaving but a narrow strip of neutral territory between the Rocky Mountains and the western borders of Missouri.

CHAPTER V.

PROTESTANT MISSIONS IN OREGON.

SO much consideration has been given to the early history of Oregon because it has been thought desirable that the reader should have some knowledge of the condition of the country and its original inhabitants, and of the almost absolutely controlling influence exerted by the fur traders, particularly the Hudson Bay Company. Enough has been said to make plain the difficulties to be overcome by the missionaries who soon thereafter attempted to Christianize and civilize the Indians.

The Flatheads and Nez Percés having learned, either from members of the land expedition of Lewis and Clark or from American trappers who had visited them later, of the existence of a Supreme Being who alone was worthy of worship, and of a book from heaven for their instruction, earnestly desired that Christian teachers should be sent to expound more fully the Christian religion. After waiting long in vain for these religious guides, they at last resolved to send four of their number East, or, in their own expressive language, "to the rising sun," where, they were told, they could learn all about the All-Powerful Being and his Holy Word. The messengers made their way through forests, across rivers, and over prairies, encountering many hostile tribes, until at last they reached St. Louis, where they met General Clark, the Superintendent of Indian

Affairs for the entire Northwest, who had in 1805–6 explored the region of country whence they came. Though kindly treated by the General, who supplied them with food and clothing, and took them to the theatre and other places of entertainment, yet, so far as known, nothing was done directly to aid them in securing the object of their perilous journey of over 3000 miles; so that, when the time came for their return, they were sad at heart, as they afterward told one of their missionaries, for they had not seen nor obtained "the Book from Heaven."

It is not known how long they remained in St. Louis, but while there the older two died, leaving the others to go back to their people and report their mission unfulfilled. Taking passage on a steamer of the American Fur Company, which was starting for the upper Missouri and to a post of the Company at the mouth of the Yellowstone, they set out on their return journey. Only one reached his people, the other sickened and died on the way. Before quitting St. Louis, they made the usual ceremonial call upon General Clark, and in a farewell address one of them made known their sorrow and disappointment in the following pathetic words:

"I came to you," said he, "over a trail of many moons from the setting sun. You were the friend of my fathers, who have all gone the long way. I came with one eye partly opened, for more light for my people who sit in darkness. I go back with both eyes closed. How can I go back blind to my blind people? I made my way to you with strong arms, through many enemies and strange lands, that I might carry back much to them. I go back with both arms broken and empty. The two fathers who came with me—the braves of many winters and wars—we leave asleep here by your great water. They were tired in many moons and their moccasins wore out. My people sent me to get the white man's Book of Heaven. You took me where you allow your women to dance, as we do not ours, and the Book was not there. You took me where they worship the Great Spirit with candles, and the Book was not there. You showed me the images of good spirits and pictures of the good land beyond, but the Book was not among them. I am going back the long, sad trail to my people of the dark land. You make my feet heavy with burdens of gifts, and my moccasins will grow old in carrying them, but the Book is not among them. When I tell my poor blind people, after one more snow, in the big council, that I did not bring the Book, no word will be spoken by our old men or by our young braves. One by one they will rise up and go out in silence. My people will die in darkness, and they will go on the long path to the other hunting-grounds. No white man will go with them and no white man's Book, to make the way plain. I have no more words."

This sad complaint was heard by a young man who was present at the interview. He was deeply impressed with its painful ending. In writing to some friends in Pittsburg he mentioned the circumstances, and these friends in turn spoke to Mr. Catlin, the great naturalist and artist, who had just returned from one of his many trips to the Rocky Mountains.* Mr. Catlin wrote and

* In his "Indian Letters" Mr. Catlin thus speaks of this mission: "When I first heard of it, I could scarcely believe it, but on consulting with General Clark I was fully convinced of the fact. . . . . They had been told that our religion was better than theirs, and that they would all be lost if they did not embrace it."

inquired of General Clark as to the truth of the statement. His reply was: "It is true. The sole object of their visit was to get the Bible." With this confirmation the letter was published, and the facts became known to the Christian public.

The fact that these Indians were seeking a knowledge of the true God, and had traveled more than three thousand miles to procure a copy of the Bible, at once excited great interest in all the churches. The result was the establishment by the Missionary Board of the Methodist Episcopal Church of a mission in the Willamette valley in Oregon, under Rev. Jason Lee and his associates, in 1834; the appointment of Rev. Samuel Parker and Dr. Marcus Whitman, by the American Board of Commissioners for Foreign Missions, to explore the country in 1835, and the establishment of a mission by the same Board in 1836.

The first missionary party sent out by the Methodist Church consisted of Revs. Jason and Daniel Lee, Cyrus Shepard and P. L. Edwards. Under the escort furnished by Captain Nathaniel Wyeth of Massachusetts, who, in 1832, had taken measures to establish trade in Oregon, they crossed the mountains and reached the plain of the Snake River, known subsequently as Fort Hall. From this point they proceeded with a party of Hudson Bay traders to Fort Nez Percé, and thence to Vancouver. They made their first permanent location about sixty miles from the mouth of the Willamette, near what is now called Wheatland, and at once made the necessary preparations to engage in the benevolent work that had brought them to the country.

The mission was largely reinforced in 1837, and again

in 1839, when it consisted of twelve clergymen and their wives and families, with a large number of lay assistants—physicians, mechanics and farmers. These large reinforcements enabled them to establish additional mission stations, and to do more than ever before both for Indians and for whites. This was the period of the mission's greatest prosperity, as to both educational and strictly missionary labors. For various causes, which we cannot take space to discuss, the work languished, and in 1847 the mission was given up by the Methodist Board of Missions. Its principal school property was sold to the trustees of the Oregon Institute, and its station at the Dalles transferred to the American Board of Foreign Missions.

Rev. Samuel Parker and Marcus Whitman, M.D., who had been appointed in 1835 to explore the country west of the Rocky Mountains with a view to engaging in missionary labors among the Indians, in due course reached the American rendezvous on Green River, in company with traders connected with the American Fur Company. Here they were met by a large number of Nez Percé Indians, who had come to trade and procure supplies, and with whom it was arranged that Mr. Parker should go to their own country, while Dr. Whitman should return to the States and report to the American Board; and should the Board decide to establish a mission, procure associates and the material necessary for a station in the Nez Percé country. Accordingly, in company with the friendly Indians, Mr. Parker continued his journey and his explorations until he reached the Columbia River, where canoes were taken to Vancouver.

On the strength of Dr. Whitman's report, the American

Board resolved to enter upon the work, and instructed Rev. Dr. and Mrs. Whitman, and Rev. H. H. and Mrs. Spalding to proceed the next year to Oregon for missionary labor among the Nez Percés. Provided with a two years' supply of such materials as they would require for a residence so many thousand miles away from civilization, the missionaries made their way to Liberty Landing, on the Missouri River, where they were joined by Mr. W. H. Gray, the secular agent of the expedition.

A few days were spent at this point in procuring wagons and horses, and in packing goods for the journey. Messrs. Spalding and Gray then went with the train to Fort Leavenworth, while Dr. Whitman and the ladies ascended the river by boat and joined them there. Here again the goods were rearranged; and, while the train proceeded as before by land, the Doctor and the ladies were to continue up the river to Council Bluffs, the point from which the American Fur Company's caravan was to start that year.

This part of the plan was frustrated by the failure of the Company's boat to land at the fort, and Dr. Whitman was compelled to send forward to Mr. Gray for horses in order to overtake the train. They were thus detained so long that the Fur Company's convoy had started, and was already six days out on the plains, before they arrived at Council Bluffs. Nothing was left for them but to press on after the caravan as rapidly as possible, and they overtook it at the Pawnee village on the Loup Fork. The difficulties of such a chase will be appreciated if it is borne in mind that the missionary party were all strangers in the country, that there was no defined road, and frequently not even a trail or track except that of the buffalo.

From the Pawnee village the march was resumed to Fort Laramie, at the mouth of the Platte River, where the invariable custom had been to abandon all the wagons and transport the goods by packing them on horses and mules. But in order to secure greater comfort for the ladies, Dr. Whitman, at his urgent request, was permitted to retain one of his wagons, and the Company concluded to try the experiment of taking along a single cart. These pioneer vehicles were placed in the special charge of Dr. Whitman, who, by his fertility of resource and indomitable perseverance, brought them through, thus demonstrating the practicability of a wagon road over the Rocky Mountains, even to the head-waters of the Columbia River. This was seven years before General Fremont's celebrated overland exploration which won him the appellation of the pathfinder.

The party having arrived at what was known then as Rock Independence, word was sent forward into the mountains as to the time when the caravan might be expected at the American rendezvous on the Green River. This information brought to the camp, two days before reaching the river, a party of ten Indians and four white men, who bore a letter from Mr. Parker, informing the missionaries of his safe arrival at Walla Walla, of the kindness of the Indians to him and their apparent friendliness to all whites. A day later, and when nearing the South Pass—the line that divides the waters of the Atlantic from those of the Pacific —the mission party were greeted by the sight of a company of Nez Percé Indians who had come to welcome them, in fulfillment of a promise made to Dr. Whitman the previous year, and to aid them in their journey. The chiefs were invited to partake of the hospitality of the missionaries, "'and here began the friendship of that nation, that bound it to the American people and government through all the conflicts of subsequent years."

The rendezvous on Green River was to all intents a military camp, so constructed as to protect the goods and animals from thieves, and its inmates from being surprised by any sudden attack from hostile Indians. Three or four hundred rough mountain men and nearly 2000 Indians were gathered at this point. Among these the presence of the two ladies of the mission party—the first to brave the dangers of an overland journey—was a great novelty and apparently the source of no little gratification.

Here the missionaries met Captain Wyeth, who, it will be remembered, formed the escort for the Methodist missionaries of the previous year. He was on his return to the States, having been obliged to abandon the fur business and sell his improvements at Fort Hall to Mr. McLeod, the chief trader of the Hudson Bay Company—another instance of the uniform policy of that Company not to permit any interference with its monopoly. While the mission party were treated with consideration and kindness by the agents and men of the Company, and allowed to join the caravan in its onward march from this point, its members were given clearly to understand that the Company did not desire the presence of the mountain men, and that no encouragement would be held out to them to migrate to Oregon. If manual labor was needed for the erection of their houses or any other improvements at the contemplated mission stations, the Company preferred to furnish it, rather than have any of these men settle in the country.

Even at this early period there was a careful scrutiny of all proposed settlers; as many being excluded as possible.

From Green River the route of travel was nearly the same as the great overland route to Bear River and Soda Springs, and thence through the spurs of the mountains to the waters of Portneuf and to Fort Hall. Here all baggage was again reduced and repacked, and Dr. Whitman was strongly urged to abandon his wagon. This he refused to do, but compromised by reducing the wagon to two wheels. Though he found it a most difficult route to travel, yet he persevered and brought his cart with its precious load safely to its destination.

From the camp on Green River, where a rest of ten days was taken, the missionaries traveled under the escort of a Hudson Bay party engaged for this purpose. After leaving the English Fort Hall, they reached Salmon Falls on the 2d of August; thence they journeyed to Boise Fort and the Grand Ronde River and over the Blue Mountains to the Umatilla River. Descending the western slope of the mountains, they beheld the great valley of the Columbia spread out before them, with Mounts Hood and Adams, and the high peaks of the Cascade range looming up grandly in the distance. A few days later, in September, 1836, a little more than four months from the time they left Missouri, the party reached Fort Walla Walla on the Columbia River, having traveled, as they estimated, a distance of 2250 miles.

Their reception by the Hudson Bay Company was friendly. At the fort, too, they found a Mr. Townsend, an American naturalist, who had spent two years in that region. From him they received not only many kindnesses but much information which was of great service to them in their subsequent intercourse with the agents of the Company, and also with the Indians. His advice to them was: "The Company will be glad to have you in the country, and your influence to improve their native wives and children. As to the Indians you have come to teach, they do not want them to be any more enlightened. The Company now has absolute control over them, and that is all they require. Should the Company learn from Mr. Pambrun [their agent] or from any other source that you are here and do not comply with their regulations and treatment of the Indians, they will cut off your supplies, and leave you to perish among the Indians you are here to benefit."

The missionaries had afterward many opportunities of proving the correctness of this judgment.

Stopping here no longer than was required for rest and to prepare for the next stage of their journey, the mission party took boats on the Columbia River, and reached Fort Vancouver September 12, 1836. On the way they encountered a severe wind storm, which came near dashing the boats to pieces, and compelled them to remain in a miserable camp for three days and nights. At Vancouver, they were also cordially welcomed by the representative of the Hudson Bay Company, and their stay of a fortnight was made as pleasant as possible.

At the earnest advice of the Company, the ladies remained at the fort, while the gentlemen of the party returned to Walla Walla to select the mission stations and to build houses for the winter—the governor supplying from the Company's stores the articles needed in building, and assuring the party that it was a great pleasure to aid them in their mission work.

At this period there were, besides the projected mission of the American Board, two mission stations of the Methodist Episcopal Church located at favorable points to reach and Christianize other tribes of Indians. It was not the purpose of the respective Boards that the established missions or the one about to be established should be in any way dependent upon the Hudson Bay Company for supplies, as ample provision had been made for their necessities until such times as they could raise the means for their own subsistence. This of necessity engaged the first attention of the newcomers, and with the supplies forwarded from the East they were soon quite independent of the Company; but such was the power of this commercial monopoly, and so important its good will, that our missionaries deemed it expedient to accept aid when it was proffered them.

In choosing locations for their missions, Messrs. Whitman and Spalding were careful not to interfere with the work already begun by their Methodist brethren. By winter they had their buildings ready for their families—Dr. Whitman at Waiilatpu, December, 1837, among the Cayuse Indians, and Mr. Spalding at Lapwai, November, 1837, on Clearwater River, among the Nez Percés. At once they began their arrangements for planting their gardens and preparing for spring crops, setting an example to the Indians by their industry during the week, and on the Sabbath giving them such religious instruction as they were capable of imparting with their then imperfect knowledge of the Indian dialects. The wives of the missionaries spent a large part of their time in teaching the children.

While the missionaries were thus engaged at their respective stations, Mr. Gray, the agent of the mission, was sent to Vancouver to procure the requisite spring supplies, and to make necessary preparations for his return to the States to secure assistance for the mission. In both respects he was successful. The American Board sent back with Mr. Gray, who was accompanied by his wife, three other missionaries and their wives—Revs. E. Walker, C. Eells, and A. B. Smith, and a young man by the name of Rogers, thus making an addition of eight members to the working force. These all arrived at Dr. Whitman's station in September, 1838. The mission of the American Board now numbered thirteen in all, and the Methodist mission sixteen. The latter was located in the Willamette Valley, with an out-station at the Dalles; the former maintained three stations at Waiilatpu, Lapwai and at Tshimakain.*

Soon after the reinforcement of the American Board's mission, two Jesuit missionaries, Revs. F. A. Blanchet and Demerse, arrived at Walla Walla in the boats of the Hudson Bay Company, making Vancouver their headquarters, and visiting its different posts and stations with the transportation facilities furnished them by the Company. Almost at once the Indians began to exhibit a prejudice against the Protestant missionaries. The priests informed them that the Protestants were not teaching a true religion ; and that eventually they intended to take their lands and property from them and occupy the country themselves. Willing assistance was lent to this propaganda by the agents and other servants of the Company, some of whom became catechists to the Indians in the interest of the

*Now known as Walker's Prairie.

Roman Catholic faith, and by the resident half-breeds, descendants of Frenchmen who had married Indian wives, and who were bigoted Romanists, and as unscrupulous as bigoted.

Meanwhile the Protestant missionaries were doing all they could to improve both the material and the spiritual condition of the Indians—teaching them to cultivate their lands and occupy them permanently, instructing their children from books already prepared in the Indian tongue, and on the Sabbath inculcating the principles of the gospel. In their annual report to the Board at Boston, in 1838, the missionaries represent the Nez Percé language as so easy of acquisition that, within four or five months after their settlement in the country, they were able to hold intercourse with the Indians in it on all common topics; and, further, that "since that time they have formed an alphabet and prepared a small elementary book in it; other books are in a state of preparation." The same report stated that the Indians of neighboring tribes were eager for missionaries, and that Mr. Gray was sent East for helpers, the opinion of the mission being that fifty missionaries and assistants were needed. In 1842 the *Missionary Herald* said: "A second book in the Nez Percé language, of fifty-six pages, has been prepared and 800 copies printed." A printing press had been procured from the Hawaiian Islands* and set up, upon which the small books required for the schools at

---

* A gift from Rev. H. Bingham's church at Honolulu; with materials accompanying it was worth $450. Mr. E. O. Hall, a printer, came along with the press, and that fall printed in the Nez Percé language the first book printed west of the Rocky Mountains.

the stations were printed, and these were gratuitously distributed to all who were willing to receive them.

The Roman Catholic priests in the meantime did all in their power to check the influence of these Protestant books and to thwart the persistent and self-denying labors of the missionaries. Their resort was to pictures ostensibly setting forth the great danger of heretical books and teachings. Other forms of opposition are referred to by the missionaries in their reports to the Board at Boston. Writing, in 1840, of the Romish priests who came from Canada, they say: "Their avowed object was to minister to the Canadian Papists in the employ of the Hudson Bay Company. But having been furnished with interpreters and facilities for traveling, they visited Fort Colville during the summer of the next year and subsequently went down to Walla Walla, where they assembled the Indians, spoke against the missionaries, said that themselves were the only men of God in the country, and persuaded a number of the Indians to receive baptism from them." Again, the annual report for 1844 states that "the papal teachers and other opposers of the mission appear to have succeeded in making them [the Indians] believe that the missionaries ought to furnish them with food and clothing and supply all their wants. Hence they make this claim and are jealous and faultfinding."

From this time forward there "was also a marked change in the feelings of most of the gentlemen of the Company" toward the Protestant missionaries; nor is it difficult to assign a sufficient cause for this change if we bear in mind the paramount and controlling purpose of the Company. If the Indians became Christianized and settled down and tilled their lands, they could not be utilized in catching the fur animals and thus add to the profits of its business. Hence, as a matter of policy entirely consonant with such a purpose, its agents favored the priests, who were subservient to its wishes and who contented themselves with teaching the Indians from a catechism for a few days or weeks at most, sprinkling them with holy water and then passing on to another place, to go through the same ceremonies, all of which left the Indians the vagabond wanderers they had been from the beginning, dependent for a living upon the chase and their traps.

The jealousy and unfriendliness of which we have just spoken was not exhibited toward the Protestant missionaries alone, but toward all persons wishing to settle in and improve the country, and especially to Americans. Even a party of forty English, Scotch and Canadian-French families who immigrated in 1841 from the Red River settlement, having been invited to locate in the Puget Sound district by the governor of the Company in order to control and outnumber the American settlers, complained bitterly of the treatment; and the more intelligent of the number removed to other districts so as to be no longer subject to the arbitrary and oppressive regulations of the Company.

The conflicting interests of the Hudson Bay Company and the actual settlers led at times to hostilities between the Americans and such Indians as were wholly under the influence of the Company's agents, and resulted in the destruction of property and the massacre of a number of the whites. It was publicly charged at the time that the

Indians were incited by the Company's employés to plunder and "murder all outside venturers upon their trading localities," the whites being regarded in all instances as the aggressors. "It has always been the policy of the Hudson Bay Company," says Hines' *Oregon*,* "to monopolize the trade of those immense regions in North America. Another feature of the policy of the Company is the course they have pursued in relation to the colonizing of the country. They have always been opposed to its settlement by any people except such as, by a strict subjection to the Company, would become subservient to their wishes. They wished to preserve the arable land for their superannuated employés, whom they kept under their absolute control, and wanted to retain them where they could use them to advantage." The same writer speaks of the inactivity of business by reason of "the domineering policy of the Hudson Bay Company."

Like testimony is given in Gray's *History of Oregon:*† "The unparalleled energy and success attending the efforts of the missionaries among these two powerful migratory tribes (Cayuses and Nez Percés) excited the jealousy of the Hudson Bay Company, and caused them to encourage the Jesuits to come to the country and locate themselves immediately in the vicinity of those missions, and use every possible influence to dissuade the Indians from attending the missionary schools, cultivating their little farms or attending in the least to any instruction, except such as was given by the priests, when they came to the Hudson Bay Company's posts for trade. The Jesuit missionary teach-

---
* Pp. 385, 386.
† P. 598.

ing did not interfere with the roving and hunting life of the Indians, while the plan of settling and civilizing them proposed, and in a measure carried out, by the American missionaries did directly interfere with the Company's fur trappers and hunters. Every Indian that became a settler or farmer had no occasion to hunt for furs to get his supplies."

Another valuable witness is Mr. Swan, who says : * "The officers of the Company also sympathized with their servants, and a deadly feeling of hatred has existed between these officers and the American immigrants. . . . . There is not a man among them who would not be glad to have had every American immigrant driven out of the country."

* *Swan's Works*, p. 381.

CHAPTER VI.

PROTESTANT MISSIONS IN OREGON, CONTINUED.

DURING all this period, and up to the year 1842, the missionaries of the American Board were prosecuting their work with commendable fidelity, and, considering the unfavorable influences which they were obliged to encounter, with remarkable success.

At the opening of the year 1839, the Indians gathered in great numbers around the mission stations then occupied, and manifested remarkable docility, both in receiving religious instruction and in adopting the habits of civilized life.

The *Missionary Herald* of 1842, represents the mission as prosperous, the schools as large, and the people as attending regularly on religious instruction. But reference is made in the Annual Report to the dissatisfaction of some of the Indians, which interfered with the prosperity of the mission, and tended to the suspension of the work of grace that had so largely prevailed. "The Indians in the vicinity of the station (Waiilatpu), instigated by a papal Indian of one of the tribes east of the mountains, had treated Dr. Whitman and Mr. Gray with a good deal of insolence and abuse, destroying some property, and demanding payment for the land, timber, fuel, and water which the missionaries used, and threatening to drive them from the country."

"About this time two Romish priests* arrived from Canada, and began to travel extensively among the Indians, and to baptize some of them; and by introducing the papal ceremonies, and by misrepresentations, seemed likely to interfere to some extent with the success of the mission." Still "the Indians were generally favorably disposed, and from eighty to one hundred families were located and cultivating the land."

Equally emphatic evidence is borne by Mr. Gray, who, as secular agent of the mission, had every opportunity for ascertaining all the facts. He says, "Before I left the Whitman station in 1842, there were 322 Indian families among the Cayuse and Nez Percé tribes that had commenced to cultivate, and were beginning to enjoy the fruits of their little farms. About 100 of them were talking about locating, and were looking for places and material for building themselves more permanent houses. We have never doubted for a moment that the Cayuse, Nez Percé, and Spokan tribes would in twenty-five years from the time the missions of the American Board were located among them (if let alone by the Hudson Bay Company and Romish priests), have become a civilized, industrious, and happy Christian people, ready to enter as honorable and intelligent citizens of our American republic." †

The English had possession of Oregon at this time as traders and settlers, and by their representations and well-laid plans were doing all they could to discourage immigration from the Eastern States. As intelligent and observant persons, the American missionaries could not fail to

---

* Messrs. Blanchet and Demerse.
† Gray's *History of Oregon*, p. 578.

discern their purposes; nor could they be expected, as patriots, to look on indifferently while another nation was endeavoring to acquire possession of this valuable territory by actual occupation.

That such was the English policy became more and more apparent to all Americans, and particularly to so careful and interested an observer as Dr. Whitman, who was soon convinced that the best if not the only way to frustrate the scheme, was to induce a still larger immigration of settlers from the United States to Oregon than could possibly be introduced by the Hudson Bay Company, with the coöperation of Sir George Simpson, the governor. His convictions on this subject were greatly strengthened during a professional visit which he paid in September, 1842, to Fort Walla Walla. Here he met at dinner the officers of the fort, a number of the chief traders of the Company, and some Jesuit priests who had recently arrived and were on their way to the interior. While the party were at table an express messenger arrived, bringing news that a large colony of immigrants from the Red River country had succeeded in crossing the mountains, and were at Fort Colville, some three hundred and fifty miles up the Columbia. This announcement was hailed with great joy by most of those present, one young priest becoming so enthusiastic that he sprang to his feet with the cry: "Hurrah for Oregon! America is too late! We have got the country!"

All that Dr. Whitman saw and heard during his stay at the fort but served to convince him more fully that the Company had not only invited these Red River Scotch and English immigrants and arranged for them to come and settle in Oregon, but that a further part of the plan was to have

Governor Simpson visit Washington and secure a final disposition of the question of the boundaries, on the basis of the most numerous and permanent settlements in the country. He at once resolved to prevent the execution of this scheme. It took him only a few hours to reach his own station, and before dismounting from his horse he briefly sketched the English plot to his brethren of the mission, ending with the announcement: "I am going to cross the Rocky Mountains and reach Washington this winter, God carrying me through, and bring out an immigration over the mountains next season, or this country is lost."

His associates, when they had recovered from their surprise, proceeded to point out the great perils of such a winter journey of five or six months, from cold, starvation, or falling into the hands of the savages, but his resolution could not be shaken. *Within twenty-four hours he started*, accompanied by Mr. A. L. Lovejoy, who had recently arrived at Waiilatpu with the immigration of that year. They took a circuitous route by way of Fort Hall, Taos and Sante Fé, and thence to Bent's Fort on the Arkansas River. Here Mr. Lovejoy stopped for the winter, having become exhausted from toil and exposure, while Dr. Whitman, in spite of intense suffering from snow-storms, extreme cold and lack of food, continued until he reached St. Louis in February, 1843. Thence he made his way to Washington, arriving on the 3d of March, precisely five months from the time of starting.

No account of this journey was left by Dr. Whitman, and in our day it would be almost impossible to comprehend the perils and privations of such an undertaking. As an indication of its many exigencies, we subjoin thrilling incidents from the narrative of the journey, compiled by Rev. H. H. Spalding from statements subsequently made by Dr. Whitman and Mr. Lovejoy:

"On that terrible 13th of January, 1843, when so many in all parts of our country froze to death, the Doctor, against the advice of his Mexican guide, left his camp in a deep gorge of the mountains of New Mexico, in the morning, to pursue his journey. But on reaching the divide, the cold becoming so intense, and the animals becoming actually maddened by the driving snows, the Doctor saw his peril, and attempted to retrace his steps, and, if possible, to find his camp, as the only hope of saving their lives. But the drifting snow had totally obliterated every trace, and the air becoming almost as dark as night by the maddening storm, the Doctor saw that it would be impossible for any human being to find camp, and, commending himself and his distant wife to his covenant-keeping God, he gave himself, his faithful guide, and animals, up to their snowy grave, which was fast closing about them. Suddenly the guide, observing the ears of one of the mules intently bent forward, sprang upon him, giving him the reins, exclaiming, 'This mule will find the camp if he can live to reach it.' The Doctor mounted another, and followed. The faithful animal kept down the divide a short distance, and then turned square down the steep mountain. Through deep snowdrifts, over frightful precipices, down, down, he pushed, unguided and unurged, as if he knew that the lives of the two men and the fate of the great expedition depended upon his endurance and his faithfulness. Entering the thick timber he stopped suddenly over a bare spot, and as the Doctor dismounted—the Mexican was too far gone—

he beheld the very fireplace of their morning camp! Two brands of fire were yet alive and smoking, and plenty of timber in reach. The buffalo hides had done much to protect the Doctor, and providentially he could move about and collect dry limbs, and soon had a rousing fire. The guide revived, but both he and the Doctor were badly frozen. They remained in this secluded hole in the mountains several days, till the cold and the storm abated.

"At another time, with another guide, on the head-waters of the Arkansas, after traveling all day in a terrible storm, they reached a small river for camp, but without a stick of wood anywhere to be had except on the other side of the stream, which was covered with ice too thin to support a man erect. The storm cleared away, and the night bid fair to be intensely cold; besides, they must have fire to prepare bread and food. The Doctor took his axe in one hand and a willow stick in the other, laid himself upon the thin ice, and spreading his legs and arms, he worked himself over on his breast, cut his wood and slid it over, and returned in the same way.

"That was the last time the Doctor enjoyed the luxury of his axe—so indispensable at that season of the year, in such a country. That night a wolf poked his nose under the foot of the bed where the axe had been placed for safe-keeping, and took it off for a leather string that was wrapped around the split helve."

Mr. Lovejoy, the companion of Dr. Whitman, has given an account of their perilous trip from Fort Hall to Fort Bent. In it he vividly describes their terrible sufferings from cold and snow, when crossing the mountains:

"From Fort Hall to Fort Uintah we met with terribly

severe weather. The deep snows caused us to lose much time. Here we took a new guide for Fort Uncompahgre, on Grand River, in Spanish country. Passing over high mountains, we encountered a terrible snow-storm, that compelled us to seek shelter in a dark defile, and although we made several attempts, we were detained some ten days. When we got upon the mountains we wandered for days, until the guide declared he was lost, and would take us no further. This was a terrible blow to the Doctor, but he determined not to give up, and went back to the Fort for another guide, I remaining with the horses, feeding them on cotton-wood bark. The seventh day he returned. We reached, as our guide informed us, Grand River, 600 yards wide, which was frozen on either side about one-third. The guide regarded it too dangerous to cross; but the Doctor, nothing daunted, was the first to take the water. He mounted his horse, and the guide and I pushed them off the ice into the boiling, foaming stream. Away they went, completely under water, horse and all, but directly came up, and after buffeting the waves and foaming current, made for the ice on the opposite side, a long way down the stream. The Doctor leaped upon the ice and soon had his noble animal by his side. The guide and I forced in the pack animals, and followed the Doctor's example, and were soon drying our frozen clothes by a comfortable fire.

"We reached Taos in about thirty days. We suffered from intense cold, and from want of food were compelled to use the flesh of dogs, mules, or such other animals as came within our reach. We remained about fifteen days, and left for Bent's Fort, which we reached January 3d.

The Doctor left there on the 7th, at which time we parted, and I did not meet him again till in July, above Laramie, on his way to Oregon with a train of emigrants."

We are fortunate in having an account of the object of Dr. Whitman's visit to the East, and of his personal appearance on his arrival at St. Louis, from the pen of Rev. William Barrows, D.D., who chanced to be a guest in the same house: *

"The announcement of the man in the little city of twenty thousand came as a surprise and a novelty. In those times it was a rare possibility for one to come up in midwinter from Bent's Fort or Santa Fé, much more from Fort Hall and the Columbia. The Rocky Mountain men, trappers and traders, the adventurers in New Mexico, and the contractors for our military posts, gathered about Dr. Whitman for fresh news from those places of interest. . . . .

"But the Doctor was in great haste, and could not delay to talk of beaver, and Indian goods, and wars, and reservations, and treaties. He had questions, not answers. Was the Ashburton treaty concluded? Did it cover the Northwest? Where, and what, and whose did it leave Oregon? . . . . Then he had other questions for his St. Louis visitors. Was the Oregon question under discussion in Congress? Would anything important be settled before the adjournment on the 4th of March? Could he reach Washington before the adjournment? He must leave at once, and he went."

The Doctor, according to the same account, "was of medium height, more compact than spare, with a stout shoulder, and large head not much above it, covered with

* *Oregon*, p. 174.

stiff, iron-gray hair, while his face carried all the moustache and whiskers that four months had been able to put upon it." His dress consisted of "coarse fur garments and vesting, and buckskin breeches. He wore a buffalo coat, with a head-hood for emergencies in taking a storm or a bivouac nap. What with heavy fur leggings and boot-moccasins, his legs filled up well his Mexican stirrups. If memory is not at fault with me, his entire dress when on the street did not show one square inch of woven fabric."

Dr. Whitman regarded his business as of so much importance that he could not be persuaded to give more than a few days to needed rest, or to the courtesies pressed upon him. He must hasten to Washington, lest delay jeopardize the object of his journey. Parting from his friends at St. Louis, he took stage for the seat of government, which he reached on the 3d of March, 1843, and soon secured an interview with the President and other public men.

I am aware that some writers have endeavored to convince the public that the chief object of Dr. Whitman's winter journey to the East was not to induce immigration to Oregon nor to convey such information to our government as was needed in order to settle aright the question of boundaries between Great Britain and the United States. They claim that his main purpose was to visit Boston, in order to induce the American Board to countermand an order sent out that year on account of the hostile disposition shown by a few Indians, discontinuing two of the stations, and thus concentrating the missionaries for greater safety; and in confirmation they adduce the fact that his missionary associates met together in order to discuss this very question the month previous to his leaving for the East.

We know of no better way of getting at the impelling motive in this case than from the testimony of those who were co-laborers of Dr. Whitman at the time, and who heard from his own lips his reasons for the journey. These all unite in stating that his main object was to save to the United States the country west of the Rocky Mountains; that he went to Washington before he visited Boston, and that he obtained a promise from officers of the government that the pending negotiations respecting the boundary line should not be concluded until it could be shown whether or not his proposed immigration could reach the Columbia River with their animals and wagons.

Of the meeting at Waiilatpu, Rev. Cushing Eells, an associate missionary, who was present, gives the following account: "The mission was called together to consider whether or not their approval would be given to the proposed undertaking—Dr. Whitman's unyielding purpose to go east, which he had formed. At the commencement there was decided opposition, which yielded only when it became evident he would go. According to the understanding of the members of the mission, the all-controlling object of Dr. Whitman was to make a desperate effort to save this country to the United States." The same writer adds that, satisfied of the movement of the English to gain possession of the country by the introduction of actual settlers, and learning from Mr. Lovejoy, who arrived with the immigrants of this year, somewhat of the condition of Oregon matters at Washington, "Dr. Whitman saw that one way to counteract this movement was to induce a still larger immigration of Americans to come to the country. He also proposed to attend to business connected with the mission, though this was a subordinate affair, and it alone would not have induced him to go east."

This evidence, confirmed as it is by the testimony of other members of the conference, must prove conclusive to every candid mind, and settle this question, which indeed has only been raised within a few years and since most of the participants in the stirring scenes have passed away.

At Washington, Dr. Whitman obtained an early hearing from the chief officers of the government. He still wore his strange attire of buffalo and buckskin, and the evidences on his person of the sufferings he had endured from cold and hunger helped to impress all he met with his sincerity and earnestness. President Tyler, on his tendering some credentials, is said to have remarked: "Dr. Whitman, your frozen face and general appearance are all the evidence I want that you have just arrived from Oregon."

That his presence in Washington was opportune, that the information which he brought relative to our possessions on the Pacific was most valuable, cannot be questioned. Sundry ill-informed and injudicious friends, however, since his death, have made unwarranted claims as to the influence he exerted upon the questions then under consideration, respecting the boundary line west of the Rocky Mountains. They are at fault not only as to dates, but as to the treaties themselves; and they attribute motives and acts to Daniel Webster which he expressly repudiated, and to which he could not have been a party. For example, a writer in the *New York Evening Post* says: "We presume it is not generally known how near we came to losing, through executive incompetence, our just title to the whole immense region lying west of the Rocky Mountains. Neither has due honor been accorded to the brave and patriotic man (Dr. Whitman) through whose herculean exertions this great loss and sacrifice was prevented.

"Reaching Washington, he sought an interview with President Tyler and Daniel Webster, then Secretary of State, and unfolded to them distinctly what was going on. Here he learned that a treaty was almost ready to be signed, in which all this northwestern territory was to be given up to England, and we were to have in compensation greater facilities in catching fish. Dr. Whitman labored to convince Mr. Webster that he was the victim of false representations with regard to the character of the region, and told him he intended to return to Oregon with a train of immigrants. Mr. Webster, looking him fully in the eye, asked him if he would pledge himself to conduct a train of immigrants there in wagons. He promised that he would. 'Then,' said Mr. Webster, 'this treaty shall be suppressed.' Dr. Whitman, in coming on, had fixed upon certain rallying-points where immigrants might assemble to accompany him on his return. He found nearly 1000 ready for the journey. After long travel, they reached Fort Hall, a British military station, and the commandant undertook to frighten the immigrants by telling them that it was not possible for them to go through with wagons; but Dr. Whitman reassured them, and led them through to the Columbia, and the days of the supremacy of the Hudson Bay Company were numbered."*

In Gray's *History of Oregon* we find the statement : "It (the Ashburton treaty) was nearly ready to be signed, but

---

*This treaty was concluded in August, 1842, and related exclusively to the boundary line east of the Rocky Mountains.

Dr. Whitman made such representations respecting the value of the country, and its accessibility, that Mr. Webster promised the treaty should be suppressed if the Doctor would conduct a caravan through to Oregon on his return journey; which he engaged to do, and had already made his arrangements for doing."

As late as 1879, a writer in the *Atlantic Monthly* said: "Mr. Webster was at one time disposed to cede the valley of the Columbia River for the free right to fish on the British colonial coasts of the North Atlantic, Governor Simpson of the Hudson Bay Company having represented Oregon as worthless for agricultural purposes, and only valuable for its furs. Just then Dr. Whitman arrived at Washington to plead for the retention of Oregon. 'But you are too late, Doctor,' said Mr. Webster, 'for we are about to trade off Oregon for the cod fisheries.' The Doctor soon convinced the Secretary of State, however, that the valley of the Columbia was of great value, and it was retained."

Similar statements have been made by other writers, notably in the *Congregationalist* of Boston, and in the *Ladies' Repository* for 1868, by Rev. H. K. Hines, of Fort Vancouver, Washington Territory; but we are confident they cannot be substantiated.

The real facts seem to be that Dr. Whitman made this remarkable journey in the winter of 1842–43, reaching Washington, March 3, 1843. The Ashburton treaty was concluded in August, 1842, and had reference only to the boundary line east of the Rocky Mountains, extending from the Bay of Fundy to the Lake of the Woods. Mr. Robert Greenhow, in his history of Oregon and California, says: "No allusion was made to any portion of the continent west of the Rocky Mountains."*

President Tyler sent a message to Congress, December 7, 1842, in which he urged that every effort should be resorted to by the two governments to settle their respective claims. It was left out of the treaty of 1842, because it would lead to a protracted discussion, and prejudice other more pressing matters. Mr. Greenhow further states, that "nothing was said on that subject (Oregon) in the British Parliament before 1843." Dr. Whitman's representations to Mr. Webster could not, therefore, have influenced the terms of the Ashburton treaty, however greatly they may have enlightened our statesmen as to the value of our Pacific coast possessions.

The northwestern boundary line was settled by Secretary Buchanan and Hon. Richard Packenham, in June, 1846. Negotiations were commenced in August, 1844, when Hon. John C. Calhoun had charge of the State Department. Great excitement was caused by our claims to the territory as far as 54° 40' north latitude, and it was feared that a war would be the consequence.

While Mr. Webster did not negotiate this treaty, he was familiar with all the questions relative to the boundary line between the two countries west of the Rocky Mountains. They had been under discussion during his term of office. This is clear from President Tyler's message already referred to, and from the correspondence of Lord Ashburton with Mr. Webster in July, 1842, in the course of which he writes: "There is a further question of disputed boundary between Great Britain and the United States, called the

* P. 78.

northwest boundary, about which we have had some conferences."

Now there is every reason to believe that Dr. Whitman's representations, and particularly his success in safely conducting nearly 1000 immigrants, with their 200 wagons, across the mountains to the Columbia River in the summer of 1843, had a very important and confirmatory influence upon Mr. Webster and all other public men of that time. That they were in need of such information as Dr. Whitman was capable of imparting may be seen from Mr. Webster's speech in the Senate, April, 1846, in defense of the Ashburton treaty of 1842, which had been bitterly assailed: "We have heard a great deal lately," says Mr. Webster, "of the immense value and importance of the Columbia River and its navigation; but I will undertake to say that, for all purposes of human use, the St. John is worth a hundred times as much as the Columbia is or ever will be."

While the above extract shows that Mr. Webster had no proper conception as to the future value of our possessions on the Pacific coast, there is no evidence to sustain the charge that he was ever disposed to trade off any part of them for fishing privileges on the Atlantic. It is expressly stated in his own works that "the government of the United States has never offered any line south of 49° with the navigation of the Columbia, and it never will." * He asserted our right to the Columbia River in virtue of Gray's discovery in 1792.

While, then, we cannot admit all that has been claimed in this matter for Dr. Whitman, it is undeniably true that

* Vol. v, p. 73.

he rendered a most important service to his country, in diffusing correct information with respect to the climate, soil, and natural resources and capabilities of our northwestern territory, in correcting the misrepresentations of English officials and the Hudson Bay Company; and especially in demonstrating the practicability of the overland route to immigrants, by the large numbers that safely arrived in Oregon the following year. Surely his patriotic labors and his character merit better treatment from his government than they have ever yet received. Both have long rested under the obloquy heaped upon them by Jesuit priests and their agents, and this in an official document—House Executive Document No. 38—published by authority of the Thirty-fifth Congress.*

* Since the above was written, Rev. Dr. Barrows has given to the public, in the main, a discriminating article on the great service Dr. Whitman rendered his country on the Oregon question. We are pleased to see that, after a careful investigation, he bears testimony to the correctness of the facts here stated.

CHAPTER VII.

THE IMMIGRATION OF 1843.

OUR pioneer missionary having explained to many of the principal men at Washington the plans and purposes of the Hudson Bay Company and the British government, which contemplated the permanent possession of the country, and having clearly showed that this was the motive for all the false representations as to its agricultural, mineral and commercial value, he announced his intention to return to Oregon overland in the early summer with a large party of immigrants, taking along with him their wagons and horses. Then he visited Boston and reported to the American Board of Commissioners for Foreign Missions. He afterwards complained that the Board had failed to appreciate his patriotic motives, and that they also found fault with him for leaving his station without permission from the Prudential Committee at Boston.

Having disposed of what little private property he possessed in the East, Dr. Whitman speedily made his way to Missouri to join the large party of immigrants who were about to start on that long and dangerous journey. Under the circumstances, he naturally felt a great responsibility for its safety and success, as it was partly through his personal representations the previous spring, when on his way to Washington, and through reading a pamphlet in which he had set forth the practicability of the route and the desirableness of the climate, soil and productions, that many members of the party had decided to make Oregon their future home.

Meanwhile, more and better information respecting Oregon had turned the attention of the people of what was then the far West to its desirableness as a place of residence. This information was furnished by such books as Rev. Mr. Parker's and Irving's *Astoria* and by the reports and debates of Congress. Public meetings at Alton and Springfield, Ill., had increased the interest and led to concerted measures for removal; so that Dr. Whitman, on reaching the western settlements on his way east, had found preparations making for a large emigration, though it was supposed that wagons could not go beyond Fort Hall. His presence among the prospective pioneers, and his assurances that the route was practicable and that he would join them and be their pilot, had increased their number. His business at Boston and a visit to his former home, however, so delayed him that the caravan, which set out on the 20th of May under Peter H. Burnet as captain, had nearly reached the Platte River before he could overtake it. His previous experience in crossing the plains, rivers and mountains enabled him at once to render most effective service to the large company. One of the members thus speaks of the crossing of the Platte soon after his joining the party: "Those who saw him [Dr. Whitman] for three days crossing and recrossing the wide stream, swimming his horse to find the best ford, and at last heard him order the one hundred or more teams to be chained together and driven in one long line to ford for two miles that river swollen by spring floods, cheering the drivers, permitting not a moment's halt, lest they should sink in the quicksands, will never forget the man nor the deed." Another* writes: "It is no disparagement to others to say that to no other individual are the emigrants of 1843 so much indebted for the successful conclusion of their journey as to Dr. Marcus Whitman."

At Fort Hall, the most eastern depot of the Hudson Bay Company, the Company's agent, as usual, did all he could to induce the immigrants to abandon their purpose of going to Oregon, by portraying the insurmountable difficulties of the way. The route to California was practicable, he said, but not that to Oregon. Dr. Whitman assured the alarmed party that if they would only trust him he would be responsible for their safe arrival in the early fall. From this place he was obliged to proceed ahead of the train, as his professional services were required at his mission. Before leaving, however, he provided a faithful Indian guide, a Cayuse chief named Istikus, who was well acquainted with the remaining part of the road. Under his guidance the party, consisting of 875 persons, some 200 wagons and 1300 head of cattle, reached the Dalles on September 20, 1843.

This immigration had been preceded by a smaller one in 1842, numbering in men, women and children 137 souls, and having in their train a few head of cattle. Other settlers arrived by sea during this and the following year, and with the assistance obtained from the Methodist mission were soon located in comfortable homes.

* Mr. Applegate.

The influence of Americans on the Pacific coast, which had been growing yearly, had now reached such a point as to excite anew the jealousy of the Hudson Bay Company and of all favoring the supremacy of the English government. "The whole policy of the Company," says Mr. Gray, "was changed when it was known that Dr. Whitman had safely arrived in Washington and the boundary line was not settled." Dr. Whitman's own estimate of the importance of the success of the latest overland immigration was probably shared by the English. He considered that it practically settled the destiny of Oregon, as is shown by a letter he wrote in April, 1847, to the American Board. It was certainly the turning-point in the history of the Territory, for it gave the control of its civil affairs into the hands of Americans.

Previous settlers from the States were alive to what the English government was doing and were apprehensive of the result. This may be learned from a petition which they sent to Congress at so early a period as 1840, in which they state that "a surveying squadron has been on the coast for the past two years, employed in making accurate surveys of all its rivers, bays and harbors; and recently the British government is said to have made a grant to the Hudson Bay Company of all lands lying between the Columbia River and Puget Sound, and the Company is actually exercising acts of ownership over these lands and opening extensive farms upon the same. These circumstances and other acts of the Company to the same effect, and their declaration that the English government own, and will hold as its own soil, that portion of Oregon north of the Columbia River, have led your petitioners to apprehend that this is the settled policy of the English government." *

"If a settler located anywhere against the Company's will, he had to pay the forfeit. Dr. McLaughlin received orders, as the governor of this western branch of this Company, to despatch agents to Fort Hall and order them to stop the American immigration, and if possible to prevent them from crossing the Blue Mountains. If that lamented man, Dr. Marcus Whitman, had not been murdered, as well as his papers burned, we should have had the evidence which this Company feared." †

In order to counteract the influence of the Protestant missionaries, and thus indirectly hinder the settlement of the country by Americans, the Hudson Bay Company favored and assisted the Jesuit priests from the time of their arrival in Oregon, which, as before stated, was soon after the Methodist mission and that of the American Board had been established.

As has also been stated, any plan for reclaiming the Indians from their wandering life and inducing them to settle down and cultivate the soil was antagonistic to the commercial interests of the Company and to its policy of holding on to all the arable land for its numerous dependents. The Indians were manifesting a tendency to better things. Gradually they were forsaking their former nomadic inclinations and were adopting a more civilized mode of life. This made the entire country safer and each year more desirable and attractive for white immigrants. That this condition of affairs was well under way

---

* Gray, pp. 194, 195.

† Hon. S. R. Thurston, in House of Representatives.

in 1842 may be seen from the report of Rev. H. H. Spalding to Dr. White, the Indian agent for Oregon:

"I am happy to say that this people (Nez Percé) are very generally turning their attention to cultivating the soil, and raising hogs, cattle and sheep, and find a much more abundant and agreeable source of subsistence in the hoe than in their bows and their sticks for digging roots. Last season about 140 cultivated from one-fourth of an acre to four or five acres each. One chief raised 176 bushels of peas last season, 100 of corn and 400 bushels of potatoes; another, 150 of peas, 160 of corn, a large quantity of potatoes, vegetables, etc. Some forty other individuals raised each from 20 to 100 bushels of grain."*

This state of things could not long go on without seriously interfering with the schemes of the agents of the Hudson Bay Company. As the missionaries were instructing the natives in the use of the plough and other agricultural implements and furnishing them with seed, it was evident that ere long most of the arable land, which at this period was confined to the borders of the streams, would presently be either in possession of the Indians or occupied by the incoming immigrants.

The methods adopted by the Roman Catholic priests contemplated no such material results, but only the simplest instruction in the ritual observances of their church, which could be secured without a fixed residence among the Indians or any particular change in their previous mode of life. These plans naturally fell in with the policy pursued by the Company, which was "to destroy the chieftainship, cut the different tribes into smaller clans, and

* The entire report may be found in Gray's *Oregon*, chap. xxxi.

divide their interests as far as possible, so as to weaken them and render them incapable of injuring the whites."*
Accordingly, soon after the arrival of Dr. Whitman and party, the Company sent for the Roman Catholic priests Blanchet and Demerse, who established their headquarters at Vancouver. Blanchet entered the field occupied by the Methodist mission, Demerse that worked by the American Board.

It was not long before this disturbing element made itself felt. "The interpreters of the Company, being of the Roman Catholic faith, made free to inform the Indians that theirs was the true religion. The Indians soon came to the station of Dr. Whitman and informed him of what had been done, and that they had been told by the priest that his was the true religion; that what he and Mr. Spalding had been teaching them was all false, and that it was not right for the Indians to listen to them."†

The Indians were told also that the American missionaries were actuated only by greed. "While the Protestant missions," says Mr. Gray, "were struggling to improve the condition of the Indians, to teach them to cultivate their lands and become permanent settlers, and to give the Indian children a knowledge of books, the Hudson Bay Company and Jesuit priests were attempting to persuade them that the instructions given by these American or Boston missionaries were only to cover up a secret design they had to take their lands and property from them, and eventually to occupy the country themselves."‡

An endeavor was made to excite the cupidity of the

---
* Hines' *Oregon*, quoted by Gray, p. 285.
† Gray, p. 180.
‡ Gray, p. 183.

Indians by telling them that the missionaries, on first coming into their country, had promised not only to pay them for all lands required for mission purposes, but to make them yearly a present of a large amount of valuable goods. The spreaders of this story were careful not to say that such promises had been made by any of the present missionaries, for that could have been easily disproved; but the burden was laid upon Mr. Parker, who in 1835 visited the Cayuse and Nez Percé tribes, to select, at their request, mission stations among them; and the sole authority for it was a statement of old John Toupin, an interpreter of the Hudson Bay Company, who claimed that he had been employed by Mr. Parker to assist him in his intercourse with the Indians. We shall not stop now to refute this false charge, as we shall have occasion to refer to the matter further on.

Another story set afloat was that the Protestant missionaries were poisoning the Indians in order to get possession of their lands. Particularly was this charged upon Dr. Whitman, who in the kindness of his heart frequently prescribed and furnished medicines gratuitously at his station. The prevalence of the measles in a virulent form, attended with an unusual number of deaths, due chiefly to the great exposure of the sick, aroused the fears and suspicions of some of the Indians, and served the purpose of the Roman Catholic half-breeds, who were instigating them to injure their greatest benefactors.

The first serious demonstration made by the Indians against the whites, was the murder and plundering of a company of fur traders who were regarded by the Hudson Bay Company as trespassers upon their hunting rights and lands. This occurred in 1842. While the Company compelled the robbers to give up the stolen property, it profited by the affair, as it secured on its own terms the large amount of valuable furs which were recovered.

During the same year, the Indians near the missions of the American Board were very insolent and annoying. They seized one of the missionaries, Rev. Mr. Smith, and grossly insulted him, on the alleged ground that he was occupying their lands. They broke into Dr. Whitman's house, and treated him with indignity and some violence. One of them presented a loaded gun at the breast of Rev. H. H. Spalding, and menaced and abused him, stopping only short of shooting him; and before leaving, they insulted both Mrs. Whitman and Mrs. Spalding. A few days after this, they burned down the misson mill on the premises of Dr. Whitman, and all its appendages and considerable grain, damaging the mission not less than $1200 or $1500.

This and succeeding years witnessed occasional panics in the white settlements, caused by the threatening attitude of the Indians, some of whom had declared their intention to kill off the "Boston" people, meaning those from the United States. Owing to the disturbed condition of the country, and other reasons which do not fall within our present purpose, the Methodist mission was abandoned, and all its missionaries left the country.

This mission being disposed of, and no longer interfering with the commercial supremacy claimed by the Company or the religious sway of the Jesuit fathers, the latter, who had in the meantime received large reinforcements from Belgium and Canada and made extensive preparations to occupy the country, were now free to give their sole attention to the destruction of the mission stations of the American Board. The influence and the consonant policy of the Company and the priests worked out a terrible result; for at Waiilatpu, on November 29, 1847, a few of the more credulous and superstitious of the Indians, directed by Finlay, a bigoted Roman Catholic half-breed, massacred, under very revolting circumstances, Dr. and Mrs. Whitman and most of their assistants, male and female. The members of the mission who escaped were compelled to leave the country. The other persons at the station, mostly immigrants who had recently arrived and had been kindly cared for by Dr. Whitman, were taken captive and held by the Indians until ransomed by Mr. Ogden, a chief factor of the Hudson Bay Company. He also sent word to the Nez Percés to deliver up Mr. Spalding and the other whites at his station. They immediately did so, bringing them to Fort Walla Walla.

As the details of this terrible tragedy are to be found in Gray's *History of Oregon*, and in Senate Executive Document No. 37, Forty-first Congress, Third Session, it needs no further notice here. It was the culmination, so to speak, of the efforts which had been made for many years by interested parties to destroy the influence of the Protestant missions, and to prevent the country's settlement by immigrants from the States. The changed feeling of the Hudson Bay Company was manifest, as we have seen, after Dr. Whitman's signal and unexpected success in bringing through to Oregon the large immigration of 1843. The conduct of the Indians toward American settlers and American missionaries also became unmistakably hostile from this time. The labors of the Protestant missionaries were steadily counteracted, and their motives misrepresented, from the day the Jesuit fathers began working among the Roman Catholic employés of the Company.

The Indian atrocities upon the peaceful inhabitants of Waiilatpu struck terror into the hearts of all the settlements exposed to attack by the savages. Measures were taken at once for the protection of the defenseless settlers and for the punishment of the murderers, by the Legislative Assembly of Oregon. Necessary funds were provided, and an armed force was on the march for the scene of action, within twenty-four hours after the issue of the executive authority for arming the volunteers. The latter were accompanied by the governor and three peace commissioners. After several slight skirmishes with hostile Indians, the military arrived at Waiilatpu, where the commissioners called for the principal chiefs of all friendly tribes to meet them in council, and arrangements for peace were concluded.

No sooner had the brief war of powder and ball ceased, than a much fiercer war of words ensued. The friends of the missionaries, and the American settlers generally, charged the Hudson Bay Company and the Jesuit priests with being either morally responsible for the massacre, or criminally culpable in not preventing it, as they were aware of the unfriendly feelings of the Indians toward Dr. Whitman and of the threats which had been made to destroy the mission and drive away the missionaries. These charges obtained general credence in the community at the time ; not only because of the known relations and spirit of those thus held accountable, but also because "in the midst of all this fury and savage shedding of blood, not one Roman

Catholic priest, not a child or servant even of the Hudson Bay Company, nor a single person who had professed friendship for the Roman Catholic faith, was harmed in the least, while all Protestant missionaries and American citizens were either killed, or driven from that part of the country."*

* Gray, pp. 470, 532.

CHAPTER VIII.

A LONG AND BITTER CONTROVERSY.

A PROTRACTED paper controversy between British subjects and Americans, and the friends respectively of the Jesuit priests and the Protestant missionaries, followed the Whitman massacre. In the course of it, certain ugly facts were adduced as to the origin of the hostility of the Indians toward the American missionaries. The singular exemption of all Roman Catholics and the Hudson Bay Company's employés from either fear or harm of any kind, and conduct on the part of certain priests, and agents of the Company, subsequent to the massacre, would suggest, unless satisfactorily explained, that they were not only indirectly, but morally responsible for the tragedy.

Against no single individual, not connected directly with the murders, did the feeling run so high, and were charges so frequently made as against Rev. J. B. A. Brouillet, Vicar-General of Walla Walla. Deeming it necessary to defend his conduct, he wrote for the *New York Freeman's Journal* a series of articles which were afterwards collected and published in a pamphlet entitled *Protestantism in Oregon.* Most of this pamphlet was embodied in a report made to the House of Representatives in 1857, by J. Ross Browne, an agent of the Treasury Department, who had been sent to the Pacific coast to obtain information respecting "the aborigines of Oregon, and the causes of war between them and the whites."

Among other things included in this report, were Brouillet's charges that the Protestant missionaries were unwise and so far unworthy men, who had brought the vengeance of the Indians upon their own heads by their imprudent and bad conduct, and whose labors had resulted in no benefit to the natives of the country.

These accusations having taken such permanent and public form, measures were adopted to refute them, and to vindicate the character and work of the missionaries. The testimony was placed in the custody of the Indian Department at Washington, and by resolution of the Senate was printed in 1871, as Executive Document 37 of the Forty-first Congress.

Soon after the publication of this document, its statements and evidence were repeatedly assailed by Roman Catholic writers, and the friends of the Protestant missions assert that very few copies of it ever went into circulation through the usual channels of distribution. They mysteriously disappeared from the public eye, and so completely, that it has been impossible for years to obtain a single copy.

The most elaborate and carefully prepared article that has fallen under the writer's notice was published in the *Catholic World* in February, 1872. Another was published in the *Catholic Sentinel* in August, 1872. In both articles the best efforts of the writers are directed to a vindication of the priests and members of the Roman Catholic Church from all complicity in the Whitman massacre and the destruction of the Protestant missions; and their main strength is put forth to blacken the moral reputations of the missionaries and depreciate their labors in civilizing and Christianizing the Indians. It is this shameful endeavor to traduce the character and conduct of good men, rather than a wish to fasten any taint of crime upon the Jesuits, that moves us to review the charges made by Roman Catholic writers, simply making known the facts and leaving the reader to judge for himself how much responsibility to visit on the priests, and how much on the Hudson Bay Company.

The *Catholic World* article opens with a complaint of habitual misrepresentations of the Roman Catholic Church by the Protestant religious press of the country, charging its editors with "blind prejudices and reckless disregard of truth," so that "no man or woman is safe from the malice or scurrility of their pens." We can safely afford to pass such accusations unnoticed, since the editors assailed require no vindication. Nor will the writer of the article complain of our silence, for he says further on, "We scarcely consider them worthy of serious attention," and proceeds:

"But we have had recently placed before us an official document, printed at the public expense for the edification of the United States Senate—and no doubt widely circulated throughout the Union under the convenient frank of many pious members of Congress—in which are reproduced calumnies so gross, and falsehoods so glaring, that we consider it our duty not only to call public attention to it, but to demand from our rulers in Washington by what right and authority they print and circulate under official form a tissue of fabrications, misrepresentations, and even forgeries, against the religion, and the ministers of that religion, which is professed by 5,000,000 or 6,000,000 of free American citizens."

We have always understood, as before stated, that this document was not "widely circulated." If it had been, surely it would have been found in our public and private libraries, and no such difficulty experienced, as always has been, to get hold of even a single copy. The fact is, comparatively few persons know even of its existence, much less of its contents. Its sudden and strange disappearance from the public archives alone accounts for this. It would not surprise us if Protestants were charged by their enemies with its destruction.

The fact is, the Senate Document was rendered necessary by the publication of another official document (No. 38) of the House of Representatives containing false and calumnious statements. The Senate document was necessary to the vindication of the truth of history. If the Romanists could have their side of the matter published at the public expense, why should not Protestants? Moreover, the Romanists have diligently written up and widely published their side of the story in their own newspapers and monthlies, in pamphlets and books; and they have seen to it that copies of these publications were deposited in our principal public libraries, in order that they might be accessible to future historians and employed to create a favorable public sentiment. Why should they complain of an effort to present the Protestant side of the case as it is understood and believed?

The next point raised against the Senate document is that it "is composed exclusively of information supplied by

Rev. H. H. Spalding to A. B. Meacham, Superintendent of Indian Affairs.* . . . . They consist mainly of extracts from the religious press, so called; inflammatory letters from jealous and disappointed preachers, including the Rev. H. H. Spalding himself; depositions written out by that indefatigable hater with his own hand, and changed in many essential points after having been sworn to and removed from the control of the deponents; false quotations from *The Account of the Murder of Dr. Whitman*, by the Very Rev. J. B. A. Brouillet, V. G., and others' statements of the massacre," etc.

What is said here about Mr. Spalding may possibly be true to the extent that he collected and forwarded some of the matter contained in the document. But in no proper sense can he be called its author; nor do the contents of the document rest on his authority only, or chiefly. The document contains the sworn evidence of a score or more of official and private persons; extracts from the most reliable historians of that part of our country, who were personally acquainted with the circumstances; and the testimony of ecclesiastical bodies on the ground, having the best of opportunities to learn the facts from reputable witnesses still living at the time when they published their solemn verdicts. This, strange to say, is the very kind of proof our critic claims to produce in his article, so far as he can command it, to destroy the reputation of the Protestant missionaries, and to shield the Jesuit priests.

But, even supposing that the contents of the Senate document had been collected and published by Mr. Spald-

---

* The depositions of witnesses, and statements of United States and State officials.

ing, why should not this great array of evidence be entitled to an authority equal at least to that of Document 38 of the House of Representatives, which it so conclusively refutes? The latter contains sixty-six pages, fifty-three of which are taken verbatim from the account of the Whitman massacre given by Vicar-General Brouillet, one of the chief parties charged with complicity in the crime.

If the objection raised by the writer of the *Catholic World* article is valid, it must apply with much greater force to the House document than to that of the Senate. The former is almost wholly the work of one man, and he an accused man, to say nothing of its character, and the large use made of it by Mr. Browne in his report, which has led to the public charge that he "ignored the people, the country, and the government whose agent he claimed to be, and was reporting for the special benefit of the Roman religion and the British government, as these are extensively quoted as historical data from which his report and conclusions are drawn." *

The writer of the article under review also attempts to cast discredit upon much of the evidence presented in the Senate document, in order to weaken its influence on the public. But this is a vain endeavor. The testimony there given, including that of a former governor of the Territory and other United States officials, cannot be shaken, much less invalidated, by the insinuations of an anonymous magazine writer.

A special point is also made against the testimony borne by the eight ecclesiastical bodies, "claiming to represent 30,000 brother members," on the ground that they knew

* Gray's *Oregon*, p. 34.

nothing personally about that concerning which they testified, and "must of necessity have depended solely on the statements of the veracious Rev. H. H. Spalding."

The reader will notice that their dependence is said to be "solely" on Rev. Mr. Spalding; as if there were no other persons with any knowledge of the facts; or as if these intelligent bodies of men, on the ground, could not and would not have availed themselves of all opportunities to learn the truth from the many accessible and reliable sources of information then existing. They were not a class of persons likely to take things at second hand, and promulgate what had been put into their mouths to utter. To say the least, they were much more likely to know the truth of what they affirmed than a writer living 3000 miles away. But we are not surprised at the effort to cast discredit upon the testimony of these large and respectable Christian denominations, for it is very explicit and pronounced in its condemnation of the Jesuit fathers.

The article in the *Catholic World* states the issue between the Romish priests and the Protestant missionaries of Oregon in the following language:

"On the week commencing on the 29th of November, 1847, more than twenty-four years ago, a certain missionary to the Cayuse Indians, named Dr. Whitman, who had resided among them for several years, was, with his wife and twelve other Americans, brutally murdered by the savages; and it is now attempted by Spalding, who was his friend, and missionary to the Nez Percés, a neighboring tribe, to fix the guilt of this foul outrage on the missionary priests who in that year accompanied the Rt. Rev. A. M. A. Blanchet, Bishop of Nesqualy, to Oregon, and who, it is alleged, instigated the Indians to commit the deed in order to get rid of the Protestant missionaries. At the time of the slaughter, there was with others under Dr. Whitman's roof a young woman named Bewley, whom one of the chiefs desired to have for his wife; and it is also asserted that not only did the priests encourage her to yield to the Indian's wishes, but forced her from the shelter of their home and refused her any protection whatever."

It will be observed that the writer alleges that the purpose of the Senate document is to fix the guilt on the Romish priests of inciting "the Indians to commit the deed in order to get rid of the Protestant missions," and of a want of humanity toward the captives, especially the young woman. He affirms, further on in the article, that "no one for months thought of attributing it to the interference of the Catholic missionaries" until "the crazy preacher [Spalding] hinted and next broadly asserted that the Jesuits were at the bottom of the whole matter." The writer also assumes that this "slander" was effectually put to rest by "a full and authentic account of the whole transaction," which was published by Rev. Mr. Brouillet, the very priest most implicated, and republished in J. Ross Browne's report.

To weaken, and to destroy as far as possible, the evidence presented in the Senate document, the writer labors to prove that the Protestant missions in Oregon were an ignominious failure, chiefly because of the bad moral character and incompetency of the missionaries. To sustain this accusation the testimony of Captain Bonneville is adduced, who visited that region in 1832, and who describes the Indians as "immaculate in honesty and purity of purpose, and more like a nation of saints than a horde of savages."

Such antecedent high morality and piety is, as might be expected, accounted for by the fact that the Indians had "imbibed some notions of the Christian faith from Catholic missionaries and traders who have been among them." When and by what Roman Catholic missionaries had these Indians been instructed prior to the year 1832? There is not a particle of proof to sustain this statement; besides, the article goes on to state that the Roman Catholic missionaries began their labors in Oregon in 1838, six years afterwards. The only other way, then, by this writer's admission, that the Indians could have been taught their wonderful piety was by the French fur-traders and the Rocky Mountain men, who were notoriously wicked and lecherous and who oppressed and wronged them in every possible manner, using them for the indulgence of their depraved passions.

The Indians of lower Oregon, who had been longest in contact with the whites and had most to do with these pious missionary fur-traders of the Hudson Bay Company, are spoken of by all the writers of that day as having been sadly corrupted by the vices of the whites, and their numbers greatly reduced by the vile and destructive diseases which the new-comers had brought among them.

But the Nez Percés are eulogized in this article for a purpose, namely, to make it appear that the Indians were made worse rather than improved through the labors of the Protestant missionaries.

The truth respecting the Nez Percés is much more nearly told by Admiral Wilkes in his *Western America*. He represents them as "superior to other tribes in intellect and in moral qualities," but adds: "There are certain traits in their character that have hitherto neutralized, in a great measure, the zealous and well-directed efforts which have been made for their improvement. The first of these is a feeling of personal independence amounting to lawlessness, which springs naturally from their habits of life and which renders it almost impossible to reconcile them to any regular discipline or system of labor. . . . . Another trait of a similar kind is a certain fickleness of temper, which makes them liable to change their opinions and policy with every passing impulse."

Let the reader of this paragraph notice, first, its indirect but valuable endorsement of the policy of the Protestant missions; second, the difficulties the missionaries had to encounter in their efforts to persuade the Indians to settle down and engage in agricultural pursuits; and, third, the susceptibility of the Indians to outside influences.

After these Indians had had the advantages for some years of the moral and pious instructions of the fur-traders, the Protestant missionaries took up their abode among them; and instead of improving in morals and religion they sadly deteriorated in both, according to the writer in the *Catholic World*. Notwithstanding the labors and teachings of the Protestant missionaries, the natives grew worse and worse in their disposition and conduct, so that the Methodist missions had finally to be abandoned, and those of the American Board were put in the way of extinction by the massacre of Dr. Whitman by his own Indians.

It would take us too far away from our present purpose

should we pause to defend at any great length the Methodist missions, which this writer assails with the same virulence as he does those of the American Board. We are inclined to believe, from what has been published from friend and foe, that their founders were good men, actuated by high and noble aims. That they did accomplish much good, we have the evidence of the witnesses quoted in the Senate document, and of Gray, who, in his *History of Oregon*, adds that they lacked experience and perhaps some other requisites of success. Their plans or methods were not the best, as Dr. Olin,* one of the authorities cited in the article in the *Catholic World*, admits.

We must remember that, being the pioneers in this missionary work, they had many and great obstacles to surmount. They had at first to give a large part of their time to raising food to supply their own necessities and provide for those dependent upon them; this led them too largely into secular affairs, which should have been kept more subordinate to the purely spiritual. They also necessarily encountered the opposition of the Hudson Bay Company in their efforts to improve the material condition of the people among whom they labored, and the power of the Company was at the time well-nigh irresistible. To these outward influences should be added the fact that the vicious whites had introduced "loathsome diseases" among the Indians, by reason of which some of the tribes in lower Oregon were fast disappearing. Rev. Mr. Parker, who visited that region in 1835, estimated the number of Indians at 8000; but Rev. Mr. Lee,

---

*Said by the writer "to be one of them." This is an error, and shows a very slight knowledge of the subject treated.

one of the chief missionaries in 1840, could find only 6000.

The testimony of Dr. White, sub Indian agent, is also quoted in the article to show the want of success of the Methodist missions:

"The Rev. Mr. Lee and associates are doing but little for the Indians. .... With all that has been expended, without doubting the correctness of the intention, it is most manifest to every observer that the Indians of this lower country, as a whole, have been very little benefited."

It is rarely that one can find more misleading and unfair quotations than these. The writer quotes only so much as suits his object, and omits all that would show what good the missionaries were doing and why they had not accomplished more.

The reports from which the extracts are taken may be seen on pages 231 and 246 of Gray's *History of Oregon.* The first extract entire is as follows:

"The Rev. Mr. Lee and associates, from their well-conducted operations at the Dalles, upon the Columbia, and a school of some thirty scholars successfully carried forward upon the Willamet, are doing but little for the Indians; nor could great efforts produce much good among the scattered remnants of the broken tribes of this lower district, who are fast disappearing before the ravages of the most loathsome diseases."

The school referred to was known as the Oregon Mission Manual Labor School. Whether it was accomplishing the purpose of its founders may be seen from the statement of Captain W. A. Slocum, of the United States Navy, who visited it in January, 1837: "I have seen children who, two years ago, were roaming over their own native wilds in a state of savage barbarism, now, being brought within the knowledge of moral and religious instruction, becoming useful members of society, by being taught the most useful of all arts, agriculture, and all this without the slightest compulsion." So well pleased was he with the methods here pursued to civilize and permanently benefit the savages that, before leaving, he made a personal contribution of fifty dollars to the funds of the school.

Out of this humble undertaking came in 1842 the collegiate institution known as the Oregon Institute, all of whose first trustees were either Methodist missionaries or were connected with the missions of that church. The funds for the erection of the necessary buildings for the institution were derived almost wholly from the same source, many persons belonging to the Methodist mission giving "from one-fourth to one-third of all they possessed." By an act of the Oregon Legislature, the Institute became Willamette University, which has had in some years as many as 300 students in attendance in its various departments. Does this look as if these men labored in vain or as if their work were rather an injury than a blessing? What candid person can look back to the foundations which they laid and deny that the influence of this Indian mission was of inestimable value to Oregon?

The second extract in the article likewise omits all that would show the reasons for no greater success. The very next line to that quoted reads:

"They were too far gone with scrofula and venereal. But

should he (Mr. Lee) insist, as a reason for his claim,* the benefit arising to the colony and the country, I am with him heartily; and notwithstanding the claim is a valuable one, this country has been increased more by the mission operations than twice its amount in finance. . . . . It is but just to say, he and his associates are exerting a considerable and most salutary influence all abroad among us."

It is thus seen that if the reports had been honestly used by the writer in the *Catholic World*, they would not have subserved his purpose, for they show that good results did attend the labors of the Methodists, and that prominent among the obstacles which limited their influence were the vices and diseases introduced among the Indians by the pious Roman Catholic French and Canadian fur traders!

Mr. Gray, in speaking of Dr. White's reports, says: "The truth is, and was at the time Dr. White wrote, 1843, that Mr. Lee and his mission were the only persons in the Willamet valley doing anything to improve the condition of the Indians, of which their Indian school, now Willamet† University, is a permanent monument." Moreover, it must be borne in mind that Dr. White was regarded by many Oregonians as having been used constantly by the Hudson Bay Company to promote and protect its interests; his influence being employed to divide and destroy the American settlement, "as he had done that of the Methodist mission."

Justice requires that in any proper estimate of what was accomplished by the Methodist mission, prominence be given to its influence in the settlement of the country; for

---

* A claim preferred by the mission to certain lands.
† Willamette.

when the time came to organize a provisional government for the protection of the inhabitants, the Methodist mission, says a trustworthy writer, "worked nobly for this object. That mission was the centre around which all these efforts at first crystallized, and without which little, if anything, would probably have been accomplished at that early day."

The labors of the missionaries were twofold. Their first and chief aim was to civilize and Christianize the Indians; but when they saw the aborigines melting away by reason of diseases introduced among them by the pious fur traders, they naturally turned their attention to benefiting the white immigrants, to whom, as we have seen, their efforts proved a great and lasting blessing.

The author of *The River of the West*, Mrs. Victor, is quoted by the writer in the *Catholic World* as saying: "So far from benefiting the Indians, the Methodist mission became an actual injury to them." Here again occurs a most noticeable omission. The entire passage is:

"'The sudden and absolute change of habits which the Indian students were compelled to make did not agree with them. The first breaking up of the ground for making farms caused malaria, and induced much sickness among them. Many had died, and many others had gone back to their former habits. Much vice and disease had prevailed among the natives, which had been introduced by deserting sailors and other profligate adventurers.'"*

---

* *River of the West*, p. 288. But Mrs. Victor is an indifferent authority at best, for elsewhere in her book she shows that she has no proper conception of religion, or the work of missions. She says Indians cannot be taught except through material things; that the missionaries began wrong, by first teaching religion, and hence their failure. She says, too,

In this way, and with such misuse of the authorities quoted, the writer in the *Catholic World* endeavors to prove the Methodist missions a failure; and with evident self-complacency he says: " There ended the first chapter in the history of the progress and civilization of the Indians in Oregon."

On the other hand, what is the judgment of Mr. Gray, who knew all the parties, was conversant with their work, and was a resident of Oregon during almost the entire period? On page 598 of his history we read:

"The Methodist missionary influence upon the natives was good, so far as they had an opportunity to exert any. At the Dalles it was certainly good and lasting, notwithstanding the Jesuits placed a station alongside of them. The Methodists were, from the commencement of their mission, interfered with in every way possible in their efforts to improve the condition of the Indians, and induce them to cultivate their lands, and leave off the hunting of fur animals."

---

that Dr. Whitman and Rev. Dr. Parker parted, because they differed and could not get along together. This is an erroneous statement. The true reason we have given.

CHAPTER IX.

MISSIONS OF THE AMERICAN BOARD.

HAVING disposed of the Methodist missions, the writer in the *Catholic World* addresses himself to what he calls the "Presbyterian mission:"

"The Methodists having selected lower Oregon as the field of their labors, the Presbyterians chose the upper or eastern portion of the territory. They arrived in 1836, three in number, afterwards increased to twelve, and backed up by the Board of Commissioners for Foreign Missions. Dr. Marcus Whitman settled at Waiilatpu among the Cayuses and Walla Wallas, and Messrs. H. H. Spalding and W. H. Gray at Lapwai, with the Nez Percés. In 1838, the Spokane mission was established by Messrs. Walker and Ellis.* Their prospects of success were at first most brilliant. The savages received them kindly, and listened to them attentively."

And Mrs. Victor testifies that "there was no want of ardor in the Presbyterian missionaries. They applied themselves in earnest to the work they had undertaken. They were diligent in their efforts to civilize and Christianize their Indians."

Similar testimony is to be seen in Townsend's narrative, *Across the Rocky Mountains*, with respect to the fidelity of Dr. Whitman and Rev. Mr. Spalding.

* Eells.

"They appear admirably qualified for the arduous duty to which they have devoted themselves, their minds being fully alive to the mortifications and trials incident to a residence among wild Indians; but they do not shrink from the task, believing it to be their religious duty to engage in this work."

But however capable and devoted these men were, according to the writer in the *Catholic World*, they "made a fatal mistake at the very beginning, which not only reflects on their personal honesty, but shows that they knew nothing of the character of the people they came to instruct."

What was this mistake that compromised "their personal honesty"? Why, that they had promised to pay the Indians for all the lands required for mission purposes, and that "a big ship loaded with goods would come yearly to be divided among them."

Who is charged with having made such foolish promises? The missionaries? No; this is not once pretended; the assertion is made against the Rev. Mr. Parker, who, as the reader will recall, visited these tribes in 1835 to select suitable places for mission stations. Had this charge been placed to the account of the missionaries, it could easily have been refuted by scores of reputable witnesses.

On whose authority is the accusation made? Not even on Vicar-General Brouillet's, which, from his relations to the question at issue, would be sufficiently untrustworthy. It rests entirely on statements of "old" John Toupin, the Roman Catholic interpreter to Pombrun, agent of the Hudson Bay Company, made in 1848, more than twelve years afterwards. Toupin's evidence is deemed so essential that it is invariably quoted, and employed in all of the

Roman Catholic accounts of the Whitman massacre. If other witnesses would have borne like testimony, who doubts that they would have been cited?

The strong antecedent improbability that any such promises were made, all must admit. If the Indians were so anxious for religious teachers as to send a deputation all the way to St. Louis to ask for them, who can believe that they would refuse to give the missionaries all the land they needed to raise crops for subsistence? "At that time," says Mr. Gray,* "there was not a band or tribe of Indians west of the Rocky Mountains but was ready to give land to any white man who would come and live in the country. This land question, as stated by Brouillet and Ross Browne, had no part in the matter."

We have carefully examined Rev. Mr. Parker's book, in which he gives an account of his visit, but we can find not a word about the alleged promises. On the contrary, he appears to have been particularly cautious and guarded in his intercourse with the Indians. On page 78, he gives an account of his and Dr. Whitman's interview with the Flatheads and Nez Percés, and says: "We laid before them the object of our appointment, and explained to them the benevolent desires of Christians concerning them." He then speaks of their desire to have missionaries come and reside among them, and of the great promise of usefulness, as the harvest was white, etc. So far from mentioning any promise to buy land or furnish presents, he says, on page 79: "We did not call together the chiefs of the Shoshones and Utaws to propose the subject of missions among them, lest we should excite expectations which

* *Oregon*, p. 461.

would not soon be fulfilled. We were more cautious upon this subject, because it is difficult to make an Indian understand the difference between a proposal and a promise."

Again, speaking of the repeated entreaties of Indians from the Dalles, who "begged for some one to come and teach them," he says: "I could not promise, but replied that I hoped it would not be more than two snows before some one would be sent . . . . that when I returned [to the East] I would use my influence to have others come and live among them."*

With reference to Brouillet's statement, solely on the authority of "old" John Toupin, that Rev. Mr. Parker made promises to the Indians, Mr. Gray speaks most positively: "Brouillet cites Rev. Mr. Parker's first supposed or imaginary statement to the Indians, as a cause of the massacre, which we know to be false and unfounded from the six years' early acquaintance we had with those Indians, and also from the personal allusions he makes to transactions with which we were intimately acquainted, and know to be false in fact and inference.† . . . . Which promise Mr. Parker never made, and these Roman priests made up to cause difficulty with the Indians and the American missions and settlements." ‡

On page 46 of Senate Executive Document 37, in answer to the question whether "the taking of the Indians' land by the missionaries was one of the causes of the murder of Dr. Whitman and family," ex-Governor Abernathy answers: "I believe and know this to be false;" and Hon. A. Hinman answers: "The most wicked falsehood ever uttered." Rev. J. L. Griffin, who was laboring as

* Parker, p. 257.   † Gray, p. 502.   ‡ Gray, p. 511.

an independent missionary at that time in Oregon, testifies as follows: "Whitman and Spalding took no lands—only the stations they occupied and improved, as the Indians requested them, and upon which they located them on arriving in the country, in answer to a call from the Indians and as authorized by a written permit by the War Department, at Washington, dated March 1, 1836."

The testimony of Chief Joseph, of the Nez Percé tribe, may be seen in an article in the *North American Review* of March, 1878. He says: "When my father was a young man there came to the country a white man [Rev. Mr. Spalding] who talked spirit law. He won the affections of our people because he spoke good things to them. At first he did not say anything about white men wanting to settle on our lands. Nothing was said about that until about twenty years ago."

It is unquestionably true that the missionaries, including Dr. Whitman, had trouble with the Indians at various times with respect to lands. The history of the mission itself, as also the statements of Messrs. Whitman and Spalding, bear evidence to this fact. In the *Annual Report of the American Board for 1842*, page 194, we have this statement, presumably based on information furnished by the missionaries:

"A papal Indian belonging to one of the tribes east of the Rocky Mountains had so instigated some of the Cayuses that they treated Dr. Whitman and Mr. Gray with a good deal of insolence and abuse, destroying some property and demanding payment for the land, timber, fuel and water the missionaries had used, and threatening to drive them from the country."

Other instances of offered violence are on record, as also the destruction by fire of a grist mill at the Waiilatpu station.

It will be observed that the demand for payment for the land was the result of the instigation of a papal Indian, and not based on any previous promise made by the missionaries. Moreover, a renegade Delaware Indian named Tom Hill had told them that "there was nothing in religion except to make money; for they (the missionaries) only wanted to make money, and at last more Americans would come and take away their land."

But the influence of these evil-minded persons extended to comparatively few of the Indians, most of the Cayuses being sensible of the great benefits they had received from the residence of the missionaries among them. At one time, when some of them expressed dissatisfaction with Dr. Whitman, he called them together and declared his willingness to leave the country if they desired. All but a very few of the tribe were anxious to have him remain. And Mr. Geiger, who was left in charge of Dr. Whitman's station when the latter made his memorable journey to the East in 1842, was evidently in the confidence of the Indians, for they consulted him at all times and relied on what he told them. This does not look as if their hostility to the mission was very great, or as if they thought the missionaries were robbing them of their lands and giving them nothing in return. Mr. Spalding held the same position respecting the land question as did Dr. Whitman; for, according to Toupin as quoted by Brouillet, Mr. Parker had made the same promises to the Nez Percés as Dr. Whitman had to the Cayuses.

That the fears of the Indians had been aroused by evil-disposed persons and by the large numbers of immigrants who were coming into their country, admits of no doubt; and that Dr. Whitman, because of his relation to the large immigration of 1843, should have become more especially obnoxious to some of the Indians, may be freely admitted. In this sense, and to this extent, the land question may have had something to do with breaking up the mission; for it is a question that has always arisen and given trouble wherever the whites have come into contact with the aborigines.

The next effort of the writer in the *Catholic World* is to depreciate the work of the missionaries. He quotes again, for this purpose, from Mrs. Victor's book: "At each of these three stations, in 1842, there was a small body of land under cultivation, a few cattle and hogs, a flouring and saw-mill and a blacksmith's shop."

This, again, has reference solely to the material progress of the Indians, which was truly remarkable when we consider the obstacles presented by the habits of the natives, the self-interest of the white traders, and the very limited resources of the missionaries. On this latter point Rev. Mr. Griffin testifies, on page 49 of the Senate document, that "Spalding and Whitman had not a dollar salary, and were allowed by the Board to 'draw but $500 a year' for each family, with which to do everything in that 'great and terrible wilderness,' destitute of everything, 200 miles from the nearest mill and 400 from shop or store, and with that to feed, clothe, house themselves and to do all missionary work."

Four lines are next selected and quoted from a report

of six pages made by Rev. Mr. Spalding to Dr. White, the sub Indian agent, going into the details of his work: "But two natives have as yet been admitted into the church. Some ten or twelve others give pleasing evidence of having been born again." This is produced to give the impression that these were all the results accomplished by Mr. Spalding and the other missionaries. The very next paragraph would have destroyed the impression sought to be made. It is as follows:

"Concerning the schools, and congregations on the Sabbath, I will speak only of this station. The congregation varies at different seasons of the year. . . . . For a few weeks in the fall, after the people return from their buffalo hunt, and then again in the spring, the congregation numbers from 1000 to 2000.* Through the winter it numbers from 200 to 800. From July to the 1st of October, it varies from 200 to 500. . . . . The school now numbers 225 in daily attendance, half of whom are adults. Nearly all the principal men and chiefs in this vicinity, with one chief from a neighboring tribe, are members of the school. They are as industrious in school as they are on their farms. Their improvement is astonishing. . . . . About 100 are printing their own books with a pen. A good number are now so far advanced in reading and printing as to render much assistance in teaching. Their books are taken home at nights and every lodge becomes a schoolroom. Their lessons are Scripture lessons; no others (except the laws) seem to interest them. . . . . Without doubt, a school of nearly

---

* The best accounts represent the tribe as then numbering from 2000 to 4000.

the same number could be collected at Kimiah, the station above this."

This report goes on to speak of Mrs. Spalding as teaching the female scholars knitting, carding, spinning and weaving, while Mr. Spalding taught agriculture, and with what success let the same authority inform us:

"It was no small tax on my time to give lessons in agriculture. That the men of the nation (the first chiefs not excepted) rose up to labor when a few hoes and seeds were offered them, I can attribute to nothing but the unseen hand of the God of missions. That their habits are really changed is acknowledged by themselves. The men say, whereas they once did not labor with their hands, now they do; and often tell me in jesting that I have converted them into a nation of women. They are a very industrious people, and, from very small beginnings, they now cultivate their lands with much skill and to good advantage."

This was but six years from the time the missionaries first reached Oregon. In the meantime they had to build their own houses, to provide the conveniences of living, and to cultivate the soil for the subsistence of their families and dependents.

Mr. Spalding tells us, in the report from which we have already quoted, that he "had all this accumulation of duties, besides eating my own bread by the sweat of my brow."

Now, as a foil to this brief and unfair quotation of four lines from a six-page statement of details, we commend the reader to Mr. Medill's report, dated November 24, 1845, to Hon. William L. Marcy, Secretary of War. Mr.

Medill was then Agent of Indian Affairs, and he bears witness as to what was accomplished in the period of nine years: "The advancement in civilization by the numerous tribes in that remote and hitherto neglected portion of our territory, with so few advantages, is a matter of surprise. . . . . Numerous schools have grown up in their midst, at which their children are acquiring the most important and useful information. They have already advanced (especially the Nez Percé nation) to a degree of civilization that promises the most beneficial results to them and their brethren on this side of the mountains, with whom they may, and no doubt will, at no distant day be brought into intercourse. They are turning their attention to agricultural pursuits, and, with but few of the necessary utensils in their possession, already produce sufficient, in some instances, to meet their every want. Among some of the tribes hunting has been almost entirely abandoned, many individuals looking wholly to the soil for support."* The reader will observe that the above statement is directly and positively at variance with that of the article; yet the writer in the *Catholic World* has the effrontery to state: "It seems, then, that it took twelve missionaries seven years to convert two savages, at an expense of over $40,000 for one year at least."

Even if this story about two converts were true, it would be easy to find its parallel in the history of missions in other lands. The first missionary in China reported only eleven converts in twenty-seven years. From a worldly point of view, this might be counted a failure; especially

* Senate Executive Document 37, p. 15.

if we ignore, as this writer has ignored, all the preparatory and incidental work which in subsequent years brought hundreds into the Church of Christ.

Dr. Judson labored five years in India before he saw any fruits of his work. But the remarkable results which followed showed that his labors were not in vain. So the Protestant missionaries in Oregon were laying broad and permanent foundations, preparing the soil and sowing the gospel seed, which would have yielded an abundant and gracious harvest if the missionaries had not been massacred or driven away. They might have got together large numbers of the Indians, as did the priests, baptized their children, sprinkled their parents with holy water, and reported them as faithful converts and members of the Christian Church. But their method of procedure was entirely different—as widely so as Protestantism from Romanism, and the wisdom of their course was proved by its final results.

Where did this writer get his information about $40,000 expenditure in a single year by Dr. Whitman and his colleagues? After the most diligent search, we can discover nothing like it; everything, indeed, points the other way, confirming what Gen. Joel Palmer says: "In this lonely situation they [Spalding and wife] have spent the best part of their days for no other compensation than a scanty subsistence." Writing of a visit to Dr. Whitman he says:

"He took occasion to inform us of many incidents. Among other things, he related that during his residence in this country, he had been reduced to such necessity for want of food as to be compelled to slay his horse; stating that within that period (ten years) no less than thirty-two horses had been served up at his table."

To the same purport is what the *Sacramento* (Cal.) *Union* published, when reviewing the labors of these missionaries: "All these results were accomplished at an expense to the American Board of Missions of $500 per annum for each mission family; the enterprise and indefatigable industry of the missionaries did the rest with native help."*

If necessary, much additional testimony could be given showing that at the very time the missionaries are represented as having expended a large sum of money, they were so poor that they had to labor with their own hands. We can account for the misstatement only on one of two suppositions: either the writer confounds the Methodist missions with those of the American Board, or he designedly substitutes the one for the other with a slight change of figures.

The *Catholic World* article further states that the remaining four years, "the years intervening between this time and their entire discontinuance, show no converts at all. Business was entirely suspended, as far as spiritual affairs were concerned."

No proper proof is given to sustain this assertion, and on the best documentary evidence we pronounce it untrue.

The preceding years constituted a period of trial and discouragement, so much so, indeed, that serious thoughts were entertained of giving up the stations. But in the spring of 1842, affairs took a much more favorable turn. The attendance upon the schools largely increased; a series of meetings among the Nez Percés resulted in the

* *Sacramento Union*, July 10, 1869.

conversion and admission to the church of seven of their number; and the Sabbath congregations among the Cayuses were larger and more attentive. "There was abundant evidence that the truth was exerting a restraining influence over most of the Indians."

Nine Nez Percés were received into the church in 1843, and it was then expected that twenty-five or thirty others would be received in a short time, but of these we have no record. Ten more were approved for church fellowship in June, 1844; and at the same time, 200 were in Sabbath-school, and two prayer-meetings were sustained. Does this look as if "business was entirely suspended, as far as spiritual affairs were concerned"?

Owing to the massacre and the resultant war with the Indians of Oregon, Rev. Mr. Spalding was obliged to retire from his mission among the Nez Percés. But while denied the privilege of direct labors for them, his interest in their spiritual welfare remained unabated. Rev. Dr. Ellinwood, Secretary of the Presbyterian Board of Foreign Missions, of New York, who has given special attention to this subject, states that "when Mr. Spalding was threescore and ten, he was permitted to baptize nearly 700 persons in the three years ending 1874." Does this look as if the spiritual results of the mission were a failure?

The author of this article in the *Catholic World* quotes further depreciatory evidence from that unfailing thesaurus, Vicar-General Brouillet's pamphlet. The first witness called is Mr. Thomas McKay, a half-breed interpreter of the Hudson Bay Company; the second, John Baptist Gervais; the third, Dr. Poujade. We have not the means by which we can identify the last two men, but their names clearly indicate their connection with the same Company. The first two represent Dr. Whitman and Mr. Spalding as saying that they had ceased to teach the Indians because they would not listen; and these words are put into Mr. Spalding's mouth: "The Indians have been getting worse every day for two or three years back; they are threatening to turn us out of the missions. A few days ago, they tore down my fences; and I do not know what the Missionary Board of New York means to do. It is a fact that we are doing no good; when the emigration passes, the Indians run off to trade, and return worse than when we came among them."

It must be conclusive to any fair-minded man that Mr. Spalding did not give Dr. Poujade the information he says he did. It is simply incredible that the former should speak of the American Board of Commissioners of Foreign Missions, of Boston, whose missionary he was, as "the Missionary Board of New York." The reference is to the dissatisfaction shown by some Indians because the whites did not visit them more frequently for purposes of trade. This we learn from General Palmer's book, *Travels over the Rocky Mountains.**

It is not now possible to ascertain whether McKay and the rest really stated what is here reported; nor do we care. We do not regard them, or the author who quotes them, as trustworthy. There is an abundance of disinterested and reliable testimony accessible to the public to disprove all they have charged, and to show the character of the missionaries and the value of their labors; but we

* P. 130.

have not space for a tithe of it. General Palmer, after a visit to Dr. Whitman's station, says:

"The condition of the savages has been greatly ameliorated, and their improvement is chiefly attributable to the missionary residents. . . . . They recognize the change which has taken place, and are not ignorant that it has been effected by the efforts and labors of the missionaries. . . . . They have embraced the Christian religion, and appear devout in their espousal of Christian doctrines. The entire time of the missionaries is devoted to the cause for which they have forsaken their friends and kindred. Their privations and trials have been great, but they have borne them with humility and meekness, and the fruits of their devotion are now manifest, and if any class of people deserve well of their country, or are entitled to the thanks of a Christian community, it is the missionaries."*

Speaking of the Nez Percés of Mr. Spalding's mission, the same writer says:

"They have made considerable advances in cultivating the soil, and have large droves of horses, and many of them are raising large herds of cattle. Mr. and Mrs. Spalding have kept up a school, and many of the Indians have made great proficiency in spelling, reading and writing. Mr. Spalding has made some translations from the Scriptures, and among others from the book of Matthew. They (the Indians) owe much of their superior qualifications to the missionaries who are among them. Mr. Spalding and family have labored among them for ten years assiduously, and the increasing wants and demands of the

* Palmer's *Travels over the Rocky Mountains*, 1845, p. 57.

natives require an additional amount of labor. Mr. Spalding must now attend not only to raising produce for his own family, but for numerous families of Indians, to act as teacher and spiritual guide, as physician, etc."*

The *Oregon Spectator*, in its issue of July 13, 1848, contained an article from the pen of Judge A. E. Wait, saying:

"We have seen a disposition to undervalue the objects and efforts of the missionaries. This is wrong; and a moment's reflection will satisfy all of the injustice of imputing selfish motives to the missionaries. The importance of the country as described by them brought the citizens of Oregon here. We can readily see what brought the Hudson Bay Company here. But what brought the missionaries, who, with their lives in their hands, led the way, with their wives, into the country, when it was almost unknown, and entirely unappreciated? It would appear that there is but one answer. It was the high and holy estimation which they placed upon the importance of souls, and the command of their Great Master in heaven."

Later and valuable evidence is borne by Mr. J. W. Anderson, Indian agent for the Nez Percés, in 1862, to the good done by the Protestant missions:

"Although Mr. Spalding had been absent from the tribe many years, yet they retained all the forms of worship which he had taught them. Many of them have prayers night and morning in their lodges. In my opinion, Mr. Spalding, by his own personal labors, has accomplished more good in this tribe than all the money expended by the government has been able to effect."

*P. 128.

Rev. Mr. Eells, writing of the Nez Percé and Cayuse tribes in 1855, at the time of the conclusion of the treaty of Walla Walla, says:

"All reports agreed that two or three lodges of the Cayuses, numbering about forty-five persons,* and about one-third of the three thousand Nez Percés, had kept up regular family and public worship. They sang from the Nez Percé hymn book, and read in their own language the Gospel of Matthew which had been furnished them by Mr. Spalding before the mission closed. . . . . Many of them kept up their knowledge of reading and writing so well that they took notes at the council, and made copies of the treaties and speeches, eight years after the mission closed. They were the chief agents in securing a peaceful council and the treaty. At that time they also expressed a strong desire that religious teachers should again be sent among them."

On pages 16 and 17 of the Senate document we have the following important and decisive testimony respecting Rev. Mr. Spalding, by Mr. Edward R. Geary, former Superintendent of the territory:

"His familiar acquaintance with the native language, reduced by him to a written state, several school books being prepared and portions of Scripture translated by him, and printed on the first press on this coast, the only instance of the kind, it is believed, among the Indian tribes on these Pacific shores. These books are held at this time above all price by the Nez Percés.

"His great, perhaps unparalleled success as a missionary

---

* This tribe was never very numerous, though wealthy and powerful. It had now become nearly extinct.

in Christianizing that people and introducing the usages of civilization among them during the eleven years spent with them, and until driven away in the year 1847, is attested by the superior intelligence, enterprise, and good order still characterizing and distinguishing them from the surrounding tribes. To this, hundreds of our citizens, civil and military officers, miners, travelers, and others of most reliable character, bear a uniform testimony. Among these we would name Commodore Wilkes, an eye-witness in 1841; Rev. Gustavus Hines in 1843, Gen. Joel Palmer in 1846, Colonel Steptoe, Agent Anderson, and Governor Daniels. The country, on the arrival of Mr. Spalding in 1836, was emphatically a wilderness; uncultivated, and with not a hoe, plow, or hoof of cattle; the savages starving on their meagre supply of roots and fishes, and ignorant of letters, of agriculture, of the Sabbath, and of human salvation.

"That this scene should so soon be changed, the 'desert to bud and blossom,' the fields to wave with grain, 15,000 to 20,000 bushels of grain harvested yearly by the Indians, orchards and gardens planted, cattle roving in bands, schools established, in which from 100 to 500 souls were in daily attendance, women spinning, over 100 professors adorning the Christian faith, a church organized and family altars erected, speaks volumes for the fidelity and efficiency of Mr. Spalding and his estimable wife."

CHAPTER X.

ROMAN CATHOLIC MISSIONS.

THE author of the article in the *Catholic World* assigns the year 1838 as the beginning of the Romish missions in Oregon, when Rev. Messrs. Blanchet and Demerse arrived at Walla Walla by the annual overland boats of the Hudson Bay Company. As the records show, they at once entered upon missionary work, passing from post to post of the Company, being furnished by its agents with every facility for travel. The missionaries of the American Board had begun their work eighteen months before, directing all their efforts to civilize, educate and Christianize the Indians, and to induce them to give up their roaming habits and engage in agriculture and stock-raising. This may prove slower than some other methods, but who will deny that it is better, if we wish to secure permanent and valuable results?

On the other hand, the method pursued by the Jesuit priests as described by Father DeSmet, in his *History of Roman Catholic Missions*, seems to have consisted mainly, if not wholly, in baptizing the Indians, young and old, so far as they could be induced to receive the ordinance. On page 32 of this history we are told that "Mr. Blanchet baptized all the children that were brought to him in the course of his journey;" and on page 35 that

Mr. Demerse in 1841 penetrated to Fort Langley, "and there baptized 700 children, they receiving the sacrament of regeneration." Bishop Blanchet, subsequently writing about them to the Bishop of Quebec, says, "Many of them already enjoy the fruits of regenerating grace."

A similar scene is thus described by Father DeSmet: "The children were arranged along the sea-coast; I distributed to each a small piece of paper with a name written thereon; and immediately commenced the ceremony. It was about ten o'clock in the morning, and I did not finish before night. The new Christians number 102." On page 59 we have an account of the wholesale baptism of 150 more children by this same priest, at another station; and on page 107 we read: "More than 100 were presented for baptism, and eleven old men were borne to me on skins, who seemed only waiting the regenerating waters, to depart home and repose in the bosom of their divine Saviour." On page 127 it is recorded: "I administered the sacrament of baptism to 105 persons, among whom were twenty adults. An imposing ceremony terminated the exercises of the day. Amongst a general salute from the camp, a large cross was elevated." On pages 208 and 209, Father DeSmet describes his visit to a tribe of Indians, the Pointed Hearts, with whom he remained three days, teaching a select few the Hail Mary, the Commandments and the Apostles' Creed. On the second day, he says, "I baptized all their small children and 24 adults;" and he concludes: "Nor have I elsewhere seen more convincing proofs of conversion to God."

On page 212 he speaks of Rev. Mr. Parker having, in 1836, broken down a cross which had been erected over

the grave of a child by some Catholic Iroquois,* and adds:
"Were he who destroyed it to return now, he would find
the image of Jesus Christ crucified, borne on the breasts of
more than 4000 Indians." He gives a further account on
page 224 of baptizing 190 Indians, and then again 418;
of 500 baptized the year before; of 196 on Christmas
day; then of 350 by Fathers Mengarini and Point; making a total of 1654 souls, "wrested from the power of the
devil."

What this new and patent method of wresting the savages from the power of the devil was, let the same writer
inform us, as he does on page 283, where he describes the
teaching of these Jesuits: "They (the Indians) were told
that the Sacrament of Extreme Unction had the power
not only to purify the soul, but to restore health to the
body; it did not occur to them to doubt the one more
than the other. . . . . They have great faith in the sign
of the cross. . . . . I saw a father and mother bending
over the cradle of an only son who was about to die.
They made their best efforts to suggest to him to make the
sign of the cross, and the child having raised his little
hand to his forehead, made the consoling sign and immediately expired."

The effect of such teaching is thus stated. "It is
worthy of remark that of all the adults who had not yet
received baptism, and all who united to prepare for their
first communion, not one was judged unworthy to receive
the sacrament. Their simplicity, piety, charity, and especially their faith, were admirable."

* A most unlikely story, resting probably on the evidence of some half-breed Catholic.

After this wholesale method of making converts to their church had been pursued for years by these priests, traveling from one fort to another, backed up by the powerful influence of the Hudson Bay Company, we are prepared to hear Father DeSmet claim that "6000 savages were brought within the fold of the Christian Church." P. 46.

These labors were carried on in this way during the intervening years until 1847, the year of the massacre; and what the results were twenty-eight years afterwards, we will allow Mr. Gray and Colonel Dow to tell us.

In reply to the query, What good have the missionaries done to the Indians? Mr. Gray says:* "If this question applied alone to the Jesuit missionaries brought to the country by the Hudson Bay Company, we would say unhesitatingly, None at all. What few Indians there are now in the country that have been baptized by them, and have learned the religious catechisms, are to-day more hopelessly depraved, and are really poorer and more degraded than they were at the time we visited them twenty-two years since, looking carefully at their moral and pecuniary condition then and now."

In the *Oregon Herald* of May 5, 1866, we find an article by Colonel Dow, on the Roman Catholic Mission of Cœur d'Alêne, spoken of invariably by Fathers DeSmet and Hoikin as their most successful mission west of the mountains: "From an acquaintance with twelve tribes of Indians, among whom the gospel has been preached, and the forms, mysteries, and ceremonies of the Catholic church introduced, I have failed to see a soul saved, or one single spark of Indian treachery, cruelty or barbarism

* P. 593.

extinguished. .... The balance of their virtues—stealing, drinking and supreme laziness—they possess in as large a share as they did before the heart of St. Alêne was sent among them. I would like to give a favorable portrait of this mission and its occupants if I could. I would like to say that the reverend fathers were neat, cleanly, intelligent, hospitable individuals, but there are too many by whom it would be pronounced false. I would like to say they were sowing the seed of civilization and cultivating it successfully in the untutored mind of the poor red man, but truth forbids. .... I say not these things with any reference to the Catholic church or its belief, nor am I forgetful of what I have read of the Jesuits of St. Bernard and their acts of humanity: but for the filthy, worthless, superannuated relics of Italian ignorance who have posted themselves midway between the extremes of Pacific and Atlantic civilization, acknowledging no law save that of their church, I have not the slightest particle of respect."

One of the Jesuit fathers (Joset), in the *Indian Sketches*,* page 61, confesses that it took him nearly fifteen years to master the language of the tribe far enough to "teach the children fourteen lessons in the catechism," and says that he had been constantly at it since his arrival. In very much less time the Protestant missionaries had translated large portions of the Bible into the native language, prepared school books, established schools and churches, and induced the Indians to settle and cultivate land for their own support.

The contrast between the two methods of civilization and their results is very marked, but only what the history

* A Roman Catholic publication.

of Roman Catholicism in other countries would lead us to expect. What was to be looked for from a score or more of priests running round from one post to another, administering sacraments wholesale to the savages and occasionally stopping long enough to get them to memorize a few lessons from the Lyons Catechism? How could such instructions be expected to elevate, civilize and Christianize Indians more than the heathen of other countries? That they did not, there is abundant evidence; yet, were we to believe what the Jesuits have published about their Oregon missions, we should conclude that, of the forty different tribes of Indians they had visited, they had succeeded in converting nearly all, and making them pious, peaceable, humane Christians!

The testimony as to the present and abiding influences exerted upon the Indians by the Protestant missionaries is abundant and in striking contrast with that of the Roman Catholics. The last report of the Board of Indian Commissioners, says Rev. Dr. S. H. Willey in 1885, gives the following as the number of Presbyterian members: Nez Percés, Lapwai 221, Kamiah 218, Umatillas 78, Spokanes 146, Shokomish 44, Dungenes 27; the total, 734.

It will be remembered that Indian wars followed the massacre for ten years, and that it was not until 1859 that the Territory was declared open to settlement, when Rev. Mr. Spalding hastened back to the Nez Percés, who eagerly welcomed him, and through his Christian instruction and labors 694 of the tribe were received into the church.

Another resultant of the American Board's mission was the founding of Whitman College, designed as a memorial of the martyred missionary. It stands near his grave, and will perpetuate both his memory and that of his associate, Rev. Dr. Cushing Eells, who laid the foundation of the institution, which, with its president and its five regular and four associate professors, is continuing the benevolent work begun more than half a century ago.

If there are such abiding fruits of the early mission work with this fading race, notwithstanding the unprecedented difficulties that it encountered, "We may well ask," says Dr. Willey, "what might it have been without them? What would our missions have been had they been undisturbed and continuous for all these years?"

The article in the *Catholic World* proceeds with a brief account of the Romanist missions in Oregon, but says that the visits of the Jesuit priests were "few and far between till the 5th of September, 1847," when, as we learn from another authority, 25 priests and 15 nuns arrived and entered vigorously upon mission work among the Indians.

This statement, the reader will notice, differs widely from that given on page 96 of the *History of Roman Catholic Missions*, by Father DeSmet: "The first mission at Nesqualy was made by Father Demerse, who celebrated the first mass in the fort on April the 22d,* the day after his arrival. His visit at such a time was forced upon him by the establishment of a Methodist mission there for the Indians."

And on page 104, DeSmet further says that Rev. Mr.

---

* This, I suppose, was in April, 1837, for Gray says that "on the arrival of Dr. Whitman and party the Hudson Bay Company sent for Blanchet and Demerse and established their headquarters at Vancouver."

Demerse's presence was needed at Vancouver "in order to oppose the efforts Minister Daniel Lee was making amongst the Indians at the fort." The evil the latter was doing is thus stated: "To deny the necessity of baptism is to deny the existence of original sin; and to deny the existence of original sin is to deny the necessity of redemption and to declare that religion is a fable, for such are the consequences following from the denial of original sin; and, alas! such was nevertheless the horrible and damnable doctrine which the Methodist ministers of Willamette preached to the Canadians."

And we learn from Brouillet, page 78, that "Fathers Blanchet and Demerse passed by Walla Walla in 1838; in 1839 Father Demerse spent three weeks in teaching the Indians and baptizing their children; and in 1840 he had made there a mission so fruitful that the Protestant missionaries had got alarmed. Father DeSmet, after visiting the Flatheads in 1840, had come and established a mission among them in 1841; and from that time down to the arrival of the Bishop, the Indians of Walla Walla and of the upper Columbia had never failed to be visited yearly, either by Father Demerse or by some of the Jesuits."

Confirmatory of this, and showing the animus of these priests toward Protestantism, we have a letter of Father DeSmet to Bishop Blanchet, dated September 28, 1841, in which he writes: "I do not doubt but that our excellent governor, Dr. McLaughlin, will give you all the assistance in his power. It is very fortunate for our holy religion that this noble-hearted man should be at the head of affairs of the honorable Hudson Bay Company. He protected it before our arrival in these regions. He still gives it his support by word and example and many favors." He then gives an account of the different Protestant missions, and adds: "In the midst of so many adversaries we try to keep our ground firmly; to increase our numbers and to visit various parts, particularly where the danger is most pressing. We also endeavor to anticipate the others and to inculcate the Catholic principles in those places where error has not yet found a footing, or even to arrest the progress of evil, to dry it up at its source. . . . . The Methodist missions are failing rapidly. . . . . This spring, Mr. Demerse withdrew from the Methodists a whole village of savages, situate at the foot of the Willamette Falls."*

It appears, then, that as early as 1837 or 1838 priests were going about baptizing children, holding missions and making many converts after their peculiar and easy methods.

The object of placing the date of the permanent occupancy of the country by Romish priests as late as 1847 is obvious; it is to have the reader believe that they were not in the country to poison the minds of the Indians against the Protestant missionaries.

The article in the *Catholic World* complains that Dr. Whitman did not receive these priests with all the cordiality he should, but "treated them with great incivility and disrespect. . . . . He refused to sell provisions to the bishop, and protested that he would not assist the missionaries unless he saw them in starvation."

So far as we can discover, this charge rests entirely on

* P. 229.

Brouillet's murder pamphlet; and it is plain that he had a powerful motive to represent Dr. Whitman in this discourteous light. But even if Dr. Whitman said and did what is here attributed to him, was that a sufficient reason to incite the Indians against him and those who fell with him? That Dr. Whitman could ever speak or act in this way, no one acquainted with him will believe for a moment. It was entirely foreign to his character and his ordinary conduct. Abundant testimony is on record as to his uniform kindness and unbounded hospitality shown to all needing these friendly offices at his hands.

We have space for only one witness on this point. Rev. Myron Eells, son of one of the missionaries, in his *History of Indian Missions*, after speaking of Dr. Whitman's valuable services to the immigrants of 1843, and of his furnishing them a guide from his mission to the Dalles free of cost, says:* "During subsequent years the hands and heart of Dr. Whitman were also full to aid the poor immigrant. A generosity fully equal to the golden rule was usually practiced, so that sometimes by the beginning of winter he found himself almost without supplies. . . . . Those too poor to proceed further sometimes wintered with him, so that at the time of his massacre there were seventy persons at his station. . . . . Of these, seven were immigrant children whose parents had died and whom he had adopted. On account of this kindness, the citizens of the Willamette were probably more ready to volunteer in order to avenge his death than they would have been for that of almost any other person on the Pacific coast."

* P. 182.

All accounts agree that Bishop Blanchet arrived at Fort Walla Walla September 5, 1847, and remained until October 26, and while there met Dr. Whitman. On October 26, Towatowe (Young Chief), a Cayuse chief, came in from hunting, and Blanchet had an interview with him, which is thus described in the pamphlet, *Murder of Dr. Whitman*, page 46: "The bishop asked him if he was disposed to receive a priest for him and his young men, telling him he could only give him one for the whole nation; and if the Cayuses wished to avail themselves of his services, they would do well to come to an understanding together concerning the location of the mission." The chief told the bishop he wished a priest, and "that he could take his house and as much land as he wanted."* So far this statement bears the impress of truth, but mark the proposal which follows from this Indian chief: "But as a means of reuniting the Cayuses, who had been heretofore divided, and in order to facilitate their religious instruction, he suggested the idea of establishing the mission near Dr. Whitman's, at the camp of Tilokaikt, as there was more land there, and it was more central."

"The previous history of this chief," says Gray, "as was given by Rev. Messrs. Hines, Perkins and Dr. White, all goes to prove that he never made such a suggestion; and no one acquainted with Indian character will believe for a moment that he did make it." †

Bishop Blanchet, either because he was not satisfied

---

* The reader will observe the willingness of the Indians to give their lands to missionaries.
† *Oregon*, p. 402.

with this proposal or for some different reason, sent for Tilokaikt, who was a relative of Towatowe, on October 29, and five days later a council was held, at which it is said the Indians offered to drive Dr. Whitman away from his station and give it to Blanchet, but the bishop declined. This rests on the statement of Thomas McKay,* plainly made to acquit the priests. Whether true or not, the fact remains that within three days Brouillet went, by order of Bishop Blanchet, to look at Tilokaikt's lands near Dr. Whitman's station; but the chief had changed his mind and was not willing to fulfill his promise and give the land. Brouillet finally accepted Young Chief's offer, quoting Tilokaikt, however, as saying: "He had no other place to give me but that of Dr. Whitman, whom he intended to send away," and his own reply: "I would not have the place of Dr. Whitman." This Cayuse Indian, who was so anxious for the priests, was engaged in the massacre, and while Dr. Whitman was still breathing, deliberately chopped his face to pieces.

That the priests and the agent of the Hudson Bay Company wanted Dr. Whitman's location, we have the evidence of Mr. John Kimzey, who was at the fort the same fall:

"During my stay of about two days, Mr. McBean,† in the presence of my wife, said: 'The fathers have offered to purchase Dr. Whitman's station, but Dr. Whitman has

---

* An Indian trader of some note in the mountains. He is a step-son of Dr. McLaughlin by an Indian mother. His father was massacred on the *Tonquin*. I have heard him declare that he will yet be known on the coast as the avenger of blood.—*Journey Across the Mountains*, p. 82, by John D. Townsend.

† Agent of the Hudson Bay Company.

refused to sell.' He said they had requested the doctor to fix his own price and they would meet it, but the doctor had refused to sell on any conditions. I asked him who he meant by the fathers. He said: 'The holy fathers, the Catholic priests.' He said the holy fathers were about to commence a mission at the mouth of the Umatilla, one in the upper part of the Umatilla, one near Dr. Whitman's station if they could not get hold of the station, one in several other places which I cannot name. He said: 'Dr. Whitman would better leave the country or the Indians will kill him; we are determined to have his station.' He further said: 'Mr. Spalding will also soon have to leave this country.' "*

On November 27, Bishop Blanchet, with his secretary and Father Brouillet, went to Umatilla, the place first offered by Young Chief. Here he received a visit from Dr. Whitman the next day. It came about through a request of two Walla Walla chiefs on the Umatilla River, that the doctor should visit the sick in their villages. Accompanied by Mr. Spalding, he started on the journey Saturday evening, November 27, arriving the same night at the lodge of Istikus, a friendly chief. Crossing the river the next day, he prescribed for the sick persons and afterwards called upon the priests at their new station. Being anxious about the sick at his own mission, he soon left for home and arrived there late in the night of the 28th or early the next morning; and on the afternoon of the 29th Dr. and Mrs. Whitman and eight others

---

* Gray, p. 463. Mr. Kimzey's deposition is confirmed by the oath of Mr. R. S. Wilcox, who heard the same or a similar statement from Mr. Kimzey in camp the night after he left Fort Walla Walla.

were murdered. One man was shot on the 30th, coming from the mill to the station; another escaped, but died of exposure or was killed by Indians; three children died; and eight days afterwards two young men were killed. Fifteen persons in all perished in the massacre. The Indians were instigated to the deed by Joe Stanfield, a Canadian Frenchman; Joe Lewis, a Canadian Indian; and Nicholas Finlay, a French half-breed—understood to be Roman Catholics.* Some of these took part in the killing, and all were busy in plundering the houses and property of the victims.

The first white man at Dr. Whitman's station after the murders was Brouillet, who came to Tilokaikt's camp on the evening of November 30, between seven and eight o'clock, and there learned of the massacre. Remaining all night at the camp, he baptized some children in the morning and then visited the scene of the tragedy, to comfort the survivors and bury the dead. Leaving on the same afternoon for his own station, he met Mr. Spalding on the way to Dr. Whitman's, informed him of the mas-

* Brouillet admits that Stanfield was a Catholic, but denies that the others were.

Lewis is said to have come from Canada with a party of priests and Frenchmen in 1847, and, being left by them at Fort Boisé, made his way to Dr. Whitman's station. While at Fort Boisé he spoke of a great overturn which would soon take place at Dr. Whitman's and in the Willamette. He made trouble among the Indians, and Dr. Whitman furnished him with shoes and clothes and induced him to leave with an immigrant who needed a teamster. Deserting the latter, he returned to Dr. Whitman's and became a leading conspirator.

Finlay was formerly in the employ of the Hudson Bay Company, and at the time was staying with the Indians near the mission. The massacre was planned in his lodge, and he afterwards claimed Mrs. Hayes as his wife. It is said that he was shot at last for murdering a guide in the employ of a company of United States troops.

sacre and advised and helped him to escape. Mr. Spalding fled, and after some days and nights of terrible suffering reached his own station and joined his wife, who in the meantime "had been protected from all harm," says Mrs. Victor, "by the faithful Nez Percés."

Three of the women who were spared from the slaughter were treated with fiendish cruelty by the Indians; and those who survived, as also the children, were finally ransomed.

CHAPTER XI.

PROLONGED CONTROVERSY OVER THE MASSACRE.

IN defending themselves from the charge of responsibility for the Whitman massacre, the accused parties offered first the testimony of an Indian who was present at the massacre, as related by one R. T. Lockwood, who elicited it by questioning. It is used to prove that the Indians had already determined to kill Dr. Whitman, before the priests came and attempted to get possession of his station.

The *Catholic World* article describes Mr. Lockwood as "an old resident of Oregon." This is not strictly true, as he only came to the State in 1851, and consequently was not a resident at the time of the murder. His moral status and his credibility as a witness we have not the means of verifying.

In a letter to Vicar-General Brouillet, published in the *Catholic Sentinel*, we have Mr. Lockwood's statement at much greater length than in the article under review. At best it is but hearsay evidence, and from an Indian who may or may not have had a share in the crime himself, and who naturally wished to exculpate his fellows. There is nothing new or important in his testimony, as he tells the usual story about the Protestant missionaries depriving the Indians of their lands,* etc. Mr. Lockwood is clearly a willing witness, and his testimony was drawn from him by Brouillet for the purpose of shielding the Romish priests.

This same letter of Lockwood's contains the statement also of a Mrs. Foster, "one of the survivors" of the murder, who expresses the opinion that Blanchet did not have anything to do with the murder, and says that he "was very kind and tender toward the survivors." The most ever asserted has been that the priests, by their teachings and by their representations of the character and purposes of the Protestant missionaries, inflamed the minds of the Indians and excited their animosity—not that they were personally implicated in the crime. How competent this witness is, and what motives induced her to express her favorable opinion, the reader must judge for himself; especially in view of the sworn evidence, already adduced, that the priests did warn the Indians against Dr. Whitman and the religion he was teaching them. †

* As to the value to be placed, in such circumstances, on the testimony of an Indian, let us hear what Mr. Brouillet says on page 86 of his account of the murder. He is speaking of the reports made by two Indians to Rev. Mr. Spalding, that the priests had told the Indians that the Protestant missionaries were poisoning them, and says: "Those reports can be of no credit, and prove nothing in the case. If in most parts of the States of the Union the testimony of Indians is never admitted as proof against the whites in any court of justice, it would be here inconsistent to make it the basis of public opinion." This is all very well; but why not apply the same rule in all similar cases? In this very instance the statements of Indians are brought out by this Mr. Lockwood to prove that the Indians had resolved upon killing Dr. Whitman before the priests came into that part of the country. The impartial reader will ask: "Is such testimony only valuable when it can be used to vilify Protestant and exculpate Roman Catholic missionaries?"

† Since the above was written, a friend has sent me a copy of the *Minutes of the Congregational Association of Oregon and Washington for*

The accused parties allege, as a second cause of the massacre, the broken promises of Rev. Mr. Parker, who told the Indians, when selecting mission stations, that he would pay for the lands occupied, and that, besides, the Indians should receive a ship-load of goods yearly. These promises had not been fulfilled, they say, but Dr. Whitman had appropriated their lands without right or compensation; hence the distrust and anger of the Indians, and their desire to requite the bad faith of the missionaries.

This will be recognized as the old, old story, resting on no better basis than "old" John Toupin, quoted from Brouillet's murder pamphlet, and already shown to be unreliable. In consonance with it, earnest efforts were made to defame the character of Dr. Whitman, in

---

1882, which contains the statement of a delegation of Umatilla Indians, made by their friend and interpreter, Dr. William McKay. These Indians were from the reservation to which the Cayuses were removed by the United States government. Their visit to the Association was to secure its influence to procure a section of land from the government for the Protestant part of the tribe, for church and school purposes, the same as the Catholics expect to obtain.

Dr. McKay says that "there is a large and increasing number of these Indians, who have declared and do declare their faith in the teachings given them by Marcus Whitman, M. D.; that they have always remembered them, and they have held meetings among themselves to talk about these things; that they have not been satisfied with the Roman Catholic teachings given on the reservation; that thirty of them have been baptized and a church organized; that they now have regular Sabbath meetings and worship; that they suffer opposition since they have held their own meetings; that they are denounced as Americans, and doomed to hell for claiming these rights of conscience, for withdrawing from the teachers set over them and for protesting against their teachings; that they are denounced for sending their children to the Government Industrial Training School at Forest Grove and told that it is a bad school; that their daughters will be ruined; that it is an American school and all who favor it will be lost."

order to show that he was capable of the perfidious acts here charged. To this end, the writer in the *Catholic World* quotes the following paragraph from Mr. Gray, whom he is careful to describe to his readers as a "brother missionary"* of Dr. Whitman, the subject of the sketch:

"A man of easy, don't-care habits, that could become all things to all men, and yet a sincere and earnest man, speaking his mind before he thought the second time, giving his views on all subjects without much consideration, correcting them when good reasons were presented, yet, when fixed in the pursuit of an object, adhering to it with unflinching tenacity. A stranger would consider him *fickle* and *stubborn*."

Here, again, we have an illustration of the defective casuistry of this Jesuit writer, in the shape of a badly garbled quotation. The italics are not Gray's, but the writer's. There is, moreover, a break in the sentence, and the quotation leaves off just where Mr. Gray brings out the good features of Dr. Whitman's character. The rest of the paragraph is as follows:

"A stranger would consider him fickle and stubborn, yet he was sincere and kind and generous to a fault, devoting every energy of his mind and body to the welfare of the Indians and objects of the mission." †

Had the writer honestly presented the entire sentence it would have ruined the object for which it was quoted, for it shows that those who knew Dr. Whitman best esteemed him most.

* Financial agent of the missions.
† *Oregon*, p. 108.

Hon. Peter H. Burnett, the first governor of California and a Catholic, in his *Recollections and Opinions of an Old Pioneer*, page 249, gives us his impressions of Dr. Whitman's character:

"I consider Dr. Whitman to have been a brave, kind, devoted and intrepid spirit, without malice and without reproach. In my best judgment, he made greater sacrifices, endured more hardships and encountered more perils for Oregon than any other one man; and his services were practically more efficient than those of any other, except, perhaps, those of Dr. Linn, United States senator from Missouri. I say *perhaps*, for I am in doubt as to which of these two men did more in effect for Oregon."

The next quotation by this writer (in the *Catholic World*) is from Mrs. Victor's *River of the West* :*

". . . . The Americans had done them much harm. Years before, had not one of their missionaries suffered several of their people and the son of their chief to be slain in his company, yet himself escaped? Had not the son of another chief (Elijah), who had gone to California to buy cattle, been killed by Americans for no fault of his own? . . . . So far as regarded the missionaries, Dr. Whitman and his associates, they were divided; yet so many looked on the doctor as an agent in promoting the settlement of the country with whites, it was thought best to drive him from the country, together with all the missionaries, *several years* before. Dr. Whitman had known that the Indians were displeased with his settlement among them. They had told him of it; they had treated him with

* P. 400.

violence; they had attempted to outrage his wife, had burned his property, and had several times warned him to leave their country or they should kill him."

We do not know the source of Mrs. Victor's information. She was not a resident of Oregon, and had no personal knowledge of what she states. It was probably derived from Brouillet, or J. Ross Browne's report, or some similar source.

This authority is again misquoted. "Several years before," at the close of the fourth sentence, belongs to the fifth, commencing "Dr. Whitman had known," etc.; and the italics are not the author's. Here we have another specimen of "the end justifying the means." This only serves to make the object clearer for which the quotation was made.

Mr. Gray says: *

"The Nez Percé chief was killed in open fight with the Sioux, on Platte River, after the party had fought three hours and killed fifteen and wounded eight of the Sioux. He was no connection of this Cayuse tribe, and only referred to here for effect."

The chief Elijah, the writer says, was "killed by Americans for no fault of his own." The facts are that he and other Indians went to California to steal horses and cattle. They ran off some horses belonging to Spaniards and Americans, first killing the Indian guards in charge of them. Elijah and Young Chief were apprehended for the crime and tried by a military court. Young Chief was acquitted on the evidence of an American whose life

* *Oregon*, p. 507.

he had saved at the time the horses were stolen, while Elijah was shot to prevent similar raids.

That this event had no connection with the massacre is very evident. The chief killed was a son of Yellow Serpent, of the Walla Walla tribe. These Indians had nothing to do with the massacre, and according to Mrs. Victor, page 415, were the only Indians who showed any kindness to the Americans on that dreadful day. Mr. McBean also states that the Walla Walla chief took no part in the murder.

We are aware that afterwards, when a council of the Indians assembled to devise measures to prevent a war with the Americans, and for this purpose sent a letter to them, the Cayuse chiefs referred to the death of Elijah as one of the wrongs they had suffered, and proposed to forget it if the Americans would not punish them for the murders at Waiilatpu. This was clearly an afterthought on their part, and perhaps suggested by others; and it only shows how destitute they were of better reasons for the act.

The object of Brouillet, who gives this matter more fully, and from whom Mrs. Victor most likely gained her knowledge, was to explain or justify the Whitman massacre. In this he so far misleads his readers as to the real causes. The origin of the unfriendly feelings by some Indians toward Dr. Whitman is clearly stated by William Geiger, Jr., who was left in charge of the mission station while Dr. Whitman was absent at Washington:

"While he was gone I was in charge of his station among the Cayuse Indians, who informed me on many occasions that the priests and half-breeds were urgent that they should drive Mr. Spalding and Dr. Whitman out of the country, so that they (the priests) could occupy the country and the places of Whitman and Spalding. I asked them on many different occasions if they wanted Messrs. Spalding and Whitman to leave their country after they had been there so long and taught them so much, both in religion and civilization, and cultivating the soil, etc. They answered: 'Oh, no; it is the priests that are continually desiring us to drive them away.'

"And, again, in 1846, the priests became very urgent, and the Catholic Indians became so noisy about the matter that the tribe held a great council about it. Dr. Whitman made them a speech. He told them his locks were getting gray. He had spent his best days in trying to do them good, but if they wished him to leave he would be ready to leave in two weeks.

"After three hours of conference they made their reply as follows:

"'When you first came to our country we knew nothing about cultivating the land and making a living in that way. We had no cattle, hogs, plows or hoes. Now we have all these, that you have assisted us to procure and taught us to use. Before you came we were always hungry in the winter; now we have plenty to eat and to spare. Formerly we knew but little of God; now we worship him every day in our families. After receiving so much we do not wish you to leave us, but to stay with us as long as you live and occupy the place that you now occupy.'"

Another form of this charge was that the missionaries were taking away the lands of the Indians.

"The fulfillment of the laws which the agent recommended for their adoption .... occasioned suspicions in the minds of the Indians generally that the whites designed the ultimate subjugation of their tribes. They saw in the laws they had adopted a deep-laid scheme of the whites to destroy them and take possession of their country. The arrival of a large party of immigrants about this time, and the sudden departure of Dr. Whitman to the United States with the avowed intention of bringing back with him as many as he could enlist for Oregon, served to hasten them to the above conclusions. .... The great complaint of the Indians was that the Boston people (Americans) designed to take away their lands and reduce them to slavery."

As this has been already refuted, it is sufficient to refer again to the well-known fact that in 1832 Indians came to St. Louis, pleading for missionaries; to their earnest entreaties of Rev. Mr. Parker in 1835, when he visited these and other tribes, that he would send them teachers; to their offer of lands to the priests; and to the testimony of Mr. Gray, who lived so long among them and who says there was not a band or tribe but was ready to give land to any white settler. There is proof positive, moreover, that the missionaries did not take nor use more land than was necessary for missionary purposes; but that the minds of the Indians were inflamed by such tales, there is no question.

The same author, Mrs. Victor, just quoted as authority to disparage the missionaries, says, pages 327 and 329:

"Dorio* (Baptiste), a half-breed, being well informed in Indian sentiments and influential as an interpreter among them, had wickedly inflamed the passions of the Indians by representing to them that it was useless making farms and building houses, as in a short time the whites would overrun their land and destroy everything, besides killing them.† . . . . The wicked Dorio still continued to poison their minds, and to stir up all the native selfishness and jealousy of the Indian character."

We have the testimony of Chief Joseph also, showing the high esteem in which the missionaries were held by most of the Indians; and that they had not said "anything about white men wanting to settle on our lands."

The third line of defense is, that the massacre was caused by the Indians' belief that Dr. Whitman was poisoning them. To substantiate this the writer in the *Catholic World* quotes from a letter of Sir James Douglas, chief factor of the Hudson Bay Company, written after the massacre, to S. N. Castle, Esq., of the Sandwich Islands.

"He hoped that time and instruction would produce a change of mind—a better state of feeling toward the mission, and he might have lived to see his hopes realized, had not the measles and dysentery, following in the train of immigrants from the United States, made frightful ravages this year in the upper country. Many Indians have been carried off through the violence of the diseases, and others through their own imprudence. The Cayuse Indians of Waiilatpu, being sufferers in this general calamity, were incensed against Dr. Whitman for not

---

* A Hudson Bay interpreter and a leader of the half-breeds.
† Hines' *Oregon* confirms this statement of Mrs. Victor.

exerting his supposed supernatural power in saving their lives. They carried this absurdity beyond the point of folly. Their superstitious minds became possessed of the horrible suspicion that he was giving poison to the sick, instead of wholesome medicine, with the view of working the destruction of the tribe, his former cruelty probably adding strength to their suspicions. Still, some of the reflecting had confidence in Dr. Whitman's integrity, and it was agreed to test the effects of the medicine he had furnished, on three of their people, one of whom was said to be in perfect health. They unfortunately died, and from that moment it was resolved to destroy the mission. It was immediately after burying the remains of these three persons that they repaired to the mission and murdered every man found there."

The information given in this letter was procured through Agent McBean, in charge of Fort Nez Percé. Another agent of the Hudson Bay Company does not hesitate to call McBean "a scoundrel;" and McBean's knowledge, it appears, was obtained from Brouillet. It was sent to Douglas by McBean's interpreter, who was at the mission when the massacre occurred, and was kept there until Brouillet had prepared an account of it for transmission to McBean, which account he carried to Sir James Douglas at Fort Vancouver. The same man was entrusted also with the secret knowledge that three parties of Indians were about to start to destroy all the other Protestant missions and American settlements in middle Oregon, including that at the Dalles; and his instructions were that he might inform the Indians, but not the whites, of what had been and what was to be done.

Hon. A. Hinman accompanied the interpreter from the Dalles, not knowing the real purpose of his visit to Fort Vancouver. He testifies that they were thirty miles from the fort when McBean's interpreter for the first time made known to him what had occurred, and confessed that "the priests, McBean, and he were bad in trying to deceive him, and have his family and people killed by the Indians."

Arriving at Vancouver, they went to Mr. Ogden's room and informed him of the massacre. His exclamation was: "Mr. Hinman, you can now see what opposition in religion will do." The three then repaired to Sir James Douglas' room and told him of the crime that had been committed, when Mr. Ogden repeated what he had previously said to Mr. Hinman. Douglas replied, "There may be other causes."

We have a more extended account of this matter on p. 40 of *Senate Executive Document 37*, being a sworn statement made by Mr. Hinman in April, 1849. This says that the Frenchman—McBean's interpreter and messenger—gave as his reason for not telling the whites: "The priests tell me not to tell you and Americans at Dalles. If I tell you, they no pardon my sins."

On going to Douglas' office Mr. Ogden said: "There, see what a war in religion has done. The good Doctor is dead. I knew there would be trouble when those priests went up."

The letters concerning the massacre were then read, and also the plans for killing other Americans, including those at the Dalles, Mr. Hinman's place of residence. When Hinman asked why the Frenchman was forbidden to tell him, Douglas replied: "You must remember, that man was in trying circumstances."

We fail to understand what is meant by this, except that there was a conflict between the Frenchman's humanity and McBean's inhumanity; for Mr. Hinman explicitly states that the Frenchman said to him: "Mr. McBean told him to say nothing about it to them at the Dalles."

When the Indians, who heard the news from the French messenger, told the whites at the Dalles, which they did after the messenger left, the whites could not believe it; for the messenger himself had told Dr. Whitman's nephew and others that he had not seen Dr. Whitman for two weeks.

McBean's letter to Sir James Douglas was afterwards demanded, and published in the *Oregon Spectator* of December 10, 1847. As it appeared there, the alleged cause of the murder is more specifically stated. It is attributed solely to the belief that Dr. Whitman was poisoning the Indians for the purpose of securing their lands; and the letter further gives currency to the story of a Mr. Rogers, who, in order to save his own life, had told the Indians that he once heard Dr. Whitman and Mr. Spalding devising measures to kill them off, and thus get possession of their lands, cattle and horses.

The charges are clearly disbelieved by the writer himself, and have all been proven false by those present at the massacre. After giving them as current stories, the letter adds: "These are only Indian reports, and no person can believe the Doctor capable of such an action, without being as ignorant and brutish as the Indians themselves."

Why, then, circulate them? They had no better

foundation than that they were told by Stanfield, Joe Lewis and Finlay. It is plain that they were given this wide currency for an evil purpose.

Sir James Douglas wrote briefly to Governor Abernethy on December 7, 1847, informing him of the massacre; and sending with his own letter that of McBean. He wrote again on December 9, to S. N. Castle, Esq., Sandwich Islands, an account for the outside world. The last letter is much fuller, and gives more extended information than was contained in the McBean letter. As we have before stated, it assigns the reason why the Indians murdered the missionaries, and repeats Rogers' statement, or what was reported as such. Here again the object is plainly to divert all suspicion from the priests and from the Hudson Bay Company.

Where did Sir James Douglas get this additional information? Undoubtedly from Brouillet. He could have procured it from no other source, and at no other time; for the interval between his two letters was only two days. The conviction is therefore forced upon us that Brouillet prepared this account the night after the massacre, and before the dead were buried, for the purpose of diverting the suspicion which the public were sure to fasten upon the priests.

Mr. Gray says that there have "always been strenuous efforts to prevent open discussion of that transaction." Sir James Douglas, it appears, procured from McBean a summary of what had taken place, while Brouillet furnished him a more carefully prepared account, which reflected severely and unjustly upon Dr. Whitman and the other missionaries, and which was sent to Mr. Castle. The transaction, moreover, shows how great was the intimacy between Sir James and Brouillet, and the Romish priests and the agents of the Hudson Bay Company. It is by such methods as these that Douglas, Brouillet and Ross Browne furnish the public with a "history of Protestant missions."

Sir James Douglas, in his letter to Mr. Castle, refers to "the horrible suspicion" of the Indians that Dr. Whitman "was giving poison to the sick, instead of wholesome medicine," and says that they selected three of their number "to test the effects of the medicine," and these dying under the treatment, they then "resolved to destroy the mission." Douglas depended on McBean and Brouillet for his information; and the latter has improved on this in his own pamphlet, where he gives as one of the reasons for killing Dr. Whitman that he was a physician, and the Indians were accustomed to kill their medicine men when their patients died under their treatment, unless a large sum of money was paid to their friends. He would have the reader infer that the Indians looked upon Dr. Whitman as one of their medicine men; yet there is not a particle of evidence, nor does Brouillet attempt to bring forward any, that the Indians regarded the Doctor in such a light.

Equally unfounded are Douglas' assertions that the Indians "were incensed against Dr. Whitman for not exerting his supposed supernatural power in saving their lives;" and that "his former cruelty probably added strength to their suspicions" respecting the poison. The former assertion lacks all semblance of proof; and the latter could only be made by persons willing to defame

Dr. Whitman, since his entire life is a refutation of the accusation of cruelty, and all his acquaintances testify that his humanity and generosity to the poor and suffering were unbounded.

If these writers had assigned the sickness and mortality which prevailed among the Indians as the reason of their hostility to the Americans, it would have been more plausible. It was a well-known fact that both measles and dysentery were introduced among them by the immigrants passing through their country; and in view of their mode of treating their sick, it is not surprising that so many died of these diseases. Their usual method of treatment was either to sweat a patient and then have him plunge into the river, or to have the medicine men hold their hands in very cold water and then apply them to the patient. Besides this, the sick were exposed to chilling rains. These facts readily account for the fatality which attended an epidemic among them, without resorting to a cruel and unsupported charge of poisoning.

That the fear caused by the occurrence of so many deaths may have had and most likely did have some influence in precipitating the massacre, can be admitted without prejudice to the missionaries. At all events it afforded an opportunity to excite the suspicions of the Indians and inflame any existing hostility. This seems to have been the opinion of Brouillet, for he gives in his pamphlet detailed statements, from several sources, of the ravages of the imported diseases among the Cayuses.

Justice, however, requires that we state what Mr. Brouillet does not, that the measles and dysentery raged just as extensively and fatally among the Indians around Fort

Colville as they did at Dr. Whitman's station; but at the Fort all was peace. Surely the facts justify Mrs. Victor in her inference* that, "in spite of all and every provocation, perhaps the fatal tragedy might have been postponed, had it not been for the evil influence of Joe Lewis" and others "who incited the Indians to murder the Americans, by telling them that they were killing them all off in order that they might possess their horses and land."

* P. 403.

CHAPTER XII.

THE AGENTS AND CAUSES OF THE MASSACRE.

THE article in the *Catholic World* lays great stress upon the alleged fact that it was Dr. Whitman's Indians who massacred him—"near neighbors of the Doctor, the worst being a member of his own household." And Brouillet says: "They were all the Doctor's own people—the Cayuses."

In contrast with this representation, we present the statement made by the Indians to Dr. William McKay, their interpreter and friend, who asked them why they "murdered Dr. Whitman if they believed him a friend and his teachings true."

"You may well ask us," they replied; "but we did not kill Dr. Whitman. The outsiders did it. Four chiefs believed their teachers, who often told them, 'Dr. Whitman is a bad man; if you follow him you will go to hell and be lost.' They conspired to kill him because of these teachings. They persuaded Te-lau-kait, the war chief [of the Cayuses], not to spare Dr. Whitman. He was there, but did not lift his hand to strike a blow or defend Dr. Whitman. He was hung, because he was with the murderers, and considered one of them. We, the other Indians, friends, were not there. We did not know what was going on. Wenapsnoot was twenty-five miles off.

The murder was a surprise to us as it was to the Americans."

To some persons the charge may seem to have considerable significance. But those most familiar with the persons and events regard this as merely showing the perfection and adroitness of the plan, which was that the killing should be done by the people whom Dr. Whitman had been laboring to benefit, and that thus the really guilty instigators of the crime might appear innocent. Mr. Gray's testimony is that the other missionaries were to be destroyed, and "that a part of the Indians at Mr. Spalding's and the Dalles were ready to engage in the same business as soon as they had their orders." This, it will be remembered, was the arrangement revealed by McBean's French interpreter to Mr. Hinman, and later to Mr. Ogden at Fort Vancouver.

The fact that these Indians were formerly friendly, and that they were the "Doctor's own people and Protestants," did not keep them from having their minds poisoned by the infamous lies told them by the Catholic half-breeds and Canadian Frenchmen.

Here, then, is the defense offered by Roman Catholic writers for the purpose of exculpating the priests from all responsibility in the massacre. As has been noticed, it consists mainly in seeking for, and assigning, reasons for the crime other than religious in their character. We have shown, as we think, that there is no valid proof of the missionaries' having said or done any of the things laid to their charge; and that the accusations of bad faith about land, poisoning, etc., rest on testimony which would not be accepted in any proper court of justice.

If this be so, then we are to look elsewhere for the causes which moved formerly friendly Indians to rise and murder their benefactors. The American settlers and the friends of the missionaries at the time charged with singular unanimity that the massacre was instigated by the Roman Catholic half-breeds and employés of the Hudson Bay Company—the former being prompted by religious zeal and bigotry which had been intensified by the presence and labors of the newly arrived priests, the latter by the fact that the missionaries civilized the Indians and encouraged white immigration, thus diminishing the profits of the fur business. This led the Company to introduce priests into the country, and to favor them in every way possible, for the purpose of crippling if not destroying the influence of Protestant missionaries, and retarding settlement by Americans; and while the priests and the Company were aware of the hostility of some of the Indians, if not of a plot formed to break up the missions, they quietly awaited the consummation, without taking measures to prevent it.

Much of the evidence relied on to sustain this view has already been adduced in the defense of the missionaries from the unjust and injurious charges made against them by Roman Catholic writers. It is necessary, however, to recall the same, and present it briefly and in order. Let us note:

I. The exemption from all danger, harm, and death, of all Roman Catholics, and all the employés of the Hudson Bay Company.

On this point we present the testimony of but two witnesses, Hon. Elwood Evans and Mr. Gray; and any one at all familiar with the history of Oregon need not be informed as to their exceptional advantages of information. Mr. Evans, in a letter to Rev. H. H. Spalding, Olympia, June 30, 1868, says:

"How naturally the query arises, 'Why is the Catholic exempt from danger; why can the Hudson Bay Company employés remain amid these scenes of blood and Indian vengeance against the white race, at peace, undisturbed, and, what is more loathsome, neutral in such a conflict; why can the priest administer the rites of his church to those Indians who are making war against Christians—even flocking to him—when you and other missionaries are fleeing for your lives because you are a missionary and an American?' Think you the conviction will not follow that the uncivilized Indian was, at best, supposing that these bloody deeds were acceptable service to those whom he continued to regard as patrons and friends? Let your narrative really illustrate that 'inasmuch as they did these things unto me' because I was an American and a Protestant, that any and all Americans at that time would have suffered like consequences, then will follow the corollary—distilled truth, the logic of history—Catholics and Britons were exempt. The American missionaries were the apostles paving the way for American occupancy—the avant-couriers of Oregon-Americanization. The Hudson Bay Company—with its auxiliaries, the Catholic missionaries—were making their last grand struggle for the sole and unlimited control of the Indian mind. They supposed they were carrying out the wishes of their teachers. See *Ogden's Speech to the Indians*, where he boldly and openly owns that 'the Indians believed they would receive the approbation of the Company.'"

Mr. Gray, in his *History of Oregon*, p. 485, comments as follows:

"What shall we say of these depositions,* and the facts asserted under the solemnity of an oath, the witnesses still living, with many others confirming the one fact, that Roman priests and Hudson Bay men, English and Frenchmen, were all safe and unharmed, while American citizens were cut down by savage hands without mercy. Without the aid of religious bigotry and the appeal to God as sending judgments upon them, not one of those simple-minded natives would ever have lifted a hand to shed the blood of their teachers or of American citizens."

Brouillet claims that the priests were in danger, and were apprehensive of violence. But we have yet to learn that a single hair of their heads was touched. Their exemption, and that of the Hudson Bay Company's men, he asserts, was owing to the fact that they had never wronged the Indians by violating promises and taking their lands, as had the American missionaries. These charges having been proved untrue, it follows that the reasons given by Brouillet for the difference of treatment accorded Catholics and Protestants have no validity.

II. The conduct of the half-breeds, Joe Lewis, Finlay, Stanfield and others, before and at the time of the massacre.

Lewis was most active in the murders, shooting down the victims, plundering the houses, and abusing helpless

---

* Sworn statements of Elam Young and others as to the causes and circumstances of the massacre.

girls. Finlay, besides counseling the savages, provided in his own house the chief rendezvous where their deviltry was concocted and matured. Brouillet, in his narrative of the murder, p. 89, offers what many persons will regard as an apology for the third villain, Stanfield, namely, that he shamed the Indians out of massacring the women and the children the day after the first murders had been committed. This rests entirely on Stanfield's own story told to Mr. Ogden at Fort Walla Walla; and Brouillet adds: "An action of that nature, if it took place, would of itself be sufficient to redeem a great many faults." Yet this wretch knew that the massacre was to take place, but neither warned the whites of their danger, nor, so far as we have any reason to believe, did the least thing to prevent it.

III. Fault has been found with the conduct of the Hudson Bay Company both before and after the massacre.

Says *Elwood Evans' History*, Chap. xix:

"The Hudson Bay Company professed neutrality. See Governor Ogden's speech to the Indians when he went to redeem the captives. See, too, what he says when he tells the Indians that they thought such acts would prove acceptable to the Company. The logic of the latter proves the outbreak to have been liable to follow the too literal appreciation of the education of the Indian mind as to their hatred of the Boston men; and neutrality in such a case is but sympathy with the wrong-doer. . . . .

"The Company's servants could travel in the hostile country in perfect safety. Any Catholic could enjoy similar immunity— *à priori* the Indians were hostile, not to whites, but to American Protestants.

"Again, there is no doubt that either the Hudson Bay Company or the Catholic missionaries could have prevented any outbreak of hostility on the part of the Indians. They failed to exercise such influence. They omitted to do a Christian, humane duty. Such an omission is as criminal, morally, as direct commission of acts inciting to hostility.

"History, therefore, ... will blame those who, provoking a storm, were not gifted with the power to control the elements, even had they the desire to do so. Nor will it excuse them because by a proffer of sympathy to stay the sacrifice of life they endeavored to relieve the captives. That Governor Ogden could relieve those captives, that the Roman clergy could stay in the midst of the hostile Indians, proves too much. The same influence, had it been properly exerted, would have avoided the massacre."

Mr. Gray says that Sir James Douglas often stated in his presence: "We" (the Hudson Bay Company) "must meet fire with fire . . . . sect with sect, settler with settler, as they had met, and were prepared to meet trader with trader."

And Hon. S. R. Thurston, in his speech in the House of Representatives in 1850, said:

"The earliest means possible were taken to wrest the whole country from us and our government. Dr. McLaughlin received orders, as the governor of this western branch of this [Hudson Bay] Company, to dispatch agents to Fort Hall and order them to stop the American immigration, and, if possible, to prevent them from crossing the Blue Mountains."

After more to the same purpose, he expresses his own

The Agents and Causes of the Massacre.

conviction in these words: "That the massacre was instigated by the Hudson Bay Company, I no more doubt, than I doubt my own existence."

This belief in the minds of many persons was greatly strengthened by the Company's unwillingness to aid in punishing the murderers. Indeed, Mr. Gray, in a pamphlet published since his history, and which may be found in the Library of the Bureau of Education, uses the following language on this point: "One-half of our male American population attempted to bring the murderers to punishment, but failed through the interference, assistance and counsels of the Hudson Bay Company and priests."

Mr. Canfield, a survivor of the massacre, takes a different view of the conduct of the Company. "Messrs. Ogden and Douglas," he says, "kept all knowledge of the massacre from the settlers in the Willamette Valley until they had concluded the purchase of the captives, for they knew that the Americans would come up to punish the Indians at once, and the latter, as soon as they heard they were coming, would kill the women and children who were their prisoners."

IV. The efforts of the Roman Catholic priests and half-breeds to destroy the influence acquired over the Indians by the Protestant missionaries, and the countenance of these efforts by the Company, as a means of breaking down the power of Americans.

In Mr. Swan's work, published in 1852, we read on page 381:

"The officers of the Company also sympathized with their servants, and a deadly feeling of hatred has existed between these officers and the American immigrants, who came across the mountains to squat upon lands they considered theirs; and there is not a man among them who would not be glad to have had every American immigrant driven out of the country."

Mr. Fitz Gerald, when opposing the extension of the charter of the Hudson Bay Company before the British Parliament in 1849, thus characterized its former principles and policy:

"A corporation who, under authority of a charter which is invalid in law, hold a monopoly in commerce and exercise a despotism in government, and have so exercised that monopoly and so wielded that power as to shut up the earth from the knowledge of man and man from the knowledge of God."

Mr. Hines, in his work on Oregon, p. 386, says of the Company:

"They have always been opposed to its settlement by any people except such as by strict subjection to the Company would become subservient to their wishes."

As to the other branch of the charge, that the priests influenced the Indians against the Protestant missionaries, we have the testimony of Mr. Spalding and Dr. Whitman. In their annual report to the American Board for 1846, Mr. Spalding ascribes his trouble with the Indians during the previous two years to a white man and a Delaware Indian from east of the mountains, "and to Romish priests, who are laboring in that quarter. . . . . Their aim seems to be to counteract the influence of the missionaries, and, if practicable, cause them to be driven from the country."

In the same report Dr. Whitman gives a summary of the

labors of the missionaries in Oregon, and says: "I look upon our location and labors here as having done enough for the cause of Christianity and civilization to compensate for all the toil and expense incurred, even without taking into account the good actually done to the Indians. A vast good has also been wrought among them." Of the disposition of the Indians, he says: "I am sure none of them wish to disturb or harm us; and more, that we are held in high estimation by them. Last fall I gave them until spring to decide whether I should leave them, as they had expressed some dissatisfaction. I was not long left in doubt, for they came forward at once and said they had no sympathy with the adherents of popery, whose ill-treatment had caused me thus to appeal to them."

Miss Bewley made the following sworn statement in December, 1848, respecting the wish and purpose of these priests to obtain the Protestant mission stations:

"When at the Umatilla, the Frenchmen [at the station with Father Blanchet] told me they were making arrangements to locate the priests—two at Mr. Spalding's as soon as Mr. Spalding got away, and two at the Dalles; and they were going to the Doctor's next week to build a house."

Mr. John Kimzey also testified, January, 1849, that Mr. McBean told him that the priests had offered to buy Dr. Whitman's station, but their offer had been declined; and that Dr. Whitman and Mr. Spalding would have to leave the country soon or the Indians would kill them; adding: "We are determined to have Dr. Whitman's station." Confirmation of this is given by Mr. F. S. Wilcox, to whom the conversation was repeated the evening after leaving the Fort.

Mr. Elam Young stated under oath in August, 1848, that when he was taken from the Doctor's saw-mill to the station one week after the massacre, for the "first ten days we were constantly told that the Catholics were coming there to establish a mission."

Mr. Daniel Young, who was at the saw-mill, some twenty miles distant, when the massacre took place, but who went to the station six days afterwards and conversed with Joe Stanfield, said that Stanfield replied, in response to a question why he was saved unless he was a Catholic: "I pass for one." Mr. Young adds that Mr. Bewley told him in Stanfield's presence that he believed Joe Lewis was one of the leaders, and that the Catholic priests were the cause of the massacre; to which Stanfield replied: "You need not believe any such thing, and you would better not let the Indians hear you say that." Soon afterward Bewley left the room, and Stanfield, turning to Mr. Young, said: "He would better be careful how he talks. If the Indians get hold of it, the Catholics may hear of it." Mr. Young subsequently cautioned Mr. Bewley, but the latter was killed two days after this conversation, at the same time with Mr. Sale.

Mr. William Geiger, Jr., in his statement respecting Dr. Whitman's trouble with the Indians and his consequent discouragements, gives as its cause "the influence of the Roman priests, exercised in talking to the Indians, and through the French half-breed, Lehai, Tom Hill, a Delaware Indian, and others;" and he adds that the Indians told him that the Roman Catholics had instructed them, "that the Protestants were leading them in wrong roads, *i. e.*, even to hell. If they followed the Suapies (Americans) they would continue to die. If they followed the Catholics, it would be otherwise with them; only now and then one would die of age."

Mr. Canfield, who was shot at the time of the massacre, but finally escaped, represents that McBean, who was in charge at Fort Walla Walla, was hostile toward the missionaries at Waiilatpu, while with the Jesuits he was on the best of terms. And he is very sure that much had been done by the people at the fort and by the Jesuits to prejudice the Indians against the Americans, and especially Dr. Whitman.

Rev. Mr. Hines, in his book, speaks frequently of the methods used to inflame the minds of the superstitious Indians against the American missionaries, and to keep them from cultivating their lands and leading settled lives. They were told that it would be of no use—that the Americans would soon come and kill them and destroy their little farms.

Governor Abernethy and Commissary-General Palmer both testify that if Romanism had never come to Oregon the massacre of Dr. Whitman would not have occurred. And Mr. J. S. Griffin, who was the editor of the *Oregon American* at the time of the massacre, says: "I am positive in my testimony that an overwhelming majority of Americans held it as proved, that the Jesuit missionaries were the procuring cause of the Whitman massacre and the other Americans who fell with him."*

To these facts and judgments we add the conclusions reached by several persons and bodies who, by reason either of their residence in Oregon at the time, or of their

* Senate Ex. Doc. 37, p. 53.

careful subsequent investigation, are entitled to have their opinions respected. The principal Protestant religious organizations of Oregon are on record on page 53 of the Senate document:

"The causes of the massacre were reducible to two, viz., the purpose of the English government or of the Hudson Bay Company to exclude American settlers from the country, and the efforts of Catholic priests to prevent the introduction of education and of Protestantism by preventing the establishment of American settlements, and that the efforts which both parties made, operating on the ignorant and suspicious minds of the savages, led to the butchery in which twenty lives were destroyed, and the most dreadful sufferings and brutal injuries inflicted on the survivors.— *Oregon Presbytery, Old School Presbyterian Church, June 22, 1869.*

"That the massacre was wholly unprovoked by Dr. Whitman, or any member or members of the mission.

"That the true cause of the massacre may be found in the course and policy pursued by the Hudson Bay Company, which was an embodiment of the British government at that time in the country, to exclude American settlers from the land, and the efforts of the Roman priests directed against the establishment of Protestantism in the country, which they hoped to accomplish by preventing its settlement by American citizens. These two things, a knowledge of which was possessed by the savages, excited them, doubtless, to perpetrate the horrid butchery, and to inflict upon the survivors the most indescribable brutalities. —*The Methodist Conference of Oregon, August, 1869.*

"That from what is regarded as evidence of the most

reliable character this Presbytery is fully convinced that the Roman clergy then occupying the country were the principal instigators of the Whitman tragedy.—*Oregon Presbytery of Cumberland Presbyterian Church, May, 1869.*

"Your committee believe, from evidence clear and sufficient to them, that these Roman priests did themselves instigate violence to the mission, resulting in the massacre, and that this document, so strangely published by Congress, with no rebutting statements accompanying it, was prepared by them to throw the blame of the massacre upon the American missionaries.—*Congregational Association of Oregon, June, 1869.*

"From personal knowledge and overwhelming testimony now before us, we, as a Presbytery, are convinced that Romanism and British influence were the main causes of the Whitman massacre, the wars that followed, and the persecuting and banishing from the country of the Protestant missionaries, destroying their property and imperiling their lives.—*Oregon Presbytery of United Presbyterian Church, 1868 and 1869.*"

The second citation will be from a pamphlet on Dr. Whitman and the settlement of Oregon, by Dr. F. F. Ellinwood, p. 11 :

"How far the Indians were instigated to the massacre is a question which will probably never be settled. That some of the Hudson Bay Company's officers and all of the Jesuit missionaries did much to prejudice the Indians against Americans, and earnestly desired their removal from the country, is beyond doubt. But that they intentionally instigated the perpetration of the murder is not proven. Charity would suggest the theory that the result of their influence was more tragic than they had anticipated."

The third citation is from the *History of Willamette Valley*, by H. O. Long, who on page 311 says:

"The Catholics cannot, however, escape a large measure of moral responsibility. They went among the Cayuses for the purpose of driving Whitman away and obtaining control of the tribe; and to accomplish this they told the Indians that Dr. Whitman was a bad man and was telling them lies, and if they did as he said they would surely go to hell. Father Brouillet ought by that time to have become sufficiently acquainted with the Indian character to know that such assertions, if they were credited, were calculated to bring about just such a tragedy as was enacted.

"The massacre was the result of four distinct causes— the dislike of Americans, the ravages of the epidemic, the poison intrigue of Joe Lewis, and the priests' denunciation of Dr. Whitman, and where the responsibility of one rests is easily seen."

Rev. Dr. William Barrows, writing to the *New York Observer*, attributes the massacre mainly to the policy and methods of the Hudson Bay Company, which "desired to hold back the wilderness, and use it only for the production of furs. It therefore kept out of it the civilized grains and grasses, the plow and hoe, and water-wheel. No Europeans were admitted excepting their own servants. All schools for the Indians were opposed, and almost all Christian missions, except the Roman Catholic." The policy of the Americans was directly the opposite of all this. Their "missions meant plows and highways and factories; it meant less fur, and corn instead, and schoolbooks." Of the English, as represented in the Company, he says that "their jealousy of the Americans took a more active and violent form. . . . . Diplomacy and trade, fraud and bloody violence, were used to keep them back."

The reader will notice that this agrees with what we have said respecting the plans of the Company to exclude Americans and keep both country and natives in their primitive state. And so strongly is Dr. Barrows impressed with this mode of accounting for the uprising of the Indians and the final massacre of Dr. Whitman, that he is not disposed to look for other causes or hold other parties to any special responsibility. Accordingly he dismisses the subject of the supposed complicity of the Roman Catholics with the remark :

"Studious and candid men, in careful survey of the facts, have gravely implicated the Jesuits, and some circumstantial evidence bears that way, and needs explaining. . . . . The question has two sides, and each has a portly amount of evidence. A careful study of the Protestant side does not satisfy me that so very grave a charge should be laid on the Catholic mission of Oregon."

We have no heart to pursue this matter further. It is no wish of ours to fasten such a crime as this upon the Romish priests, whose advent in the territory was the signal, at any rate, for strife and bloodshed. As stated before, our object has been to vindicate the characters and the work of the Protestant missionaries from the vile accusations which have been heaped upon them persistently by Roman Catholic writers. In doing this we have given the facts as nearly as they can now be ascertained from existing public documents, from histories of the country, and from the testimony of persons who either had direct knowledge of what they narrate, or obtained it from those who lived in the State at the time and were acquainted with the actors and circumstances. And if the reader draws an inference unfavorable to any of the actors in these events, and especially to the conduct and teachings of the Romish priests, it will not be owing entirely to the evidence here produced as to their moral complicity in the cruel tragedy in Oregon, but largely to the fact that the Roman Catholic Church in all its past history, when it possessed the power, has ever been a persecuting church, and regarded its mission to be either the conversion or the destruction of heretics—in other words, Protestants.

CHAPTER XIII.

SURVIVORS OF THE MASSACRE.

IT was charged, at the time of the massacre, that some of the survivors were not treated with becoming humanity by the priests or by the agents of the Hudson Bay Company.

It appears that Brouillet, after seeing the victims buried, departed the next day for his newly acquired station. Before leaving Waiilatpu, the scene of the murders, he is said to have promised the survivors that he would do all in his power to protect and assist them, but he did not keep his promise. He afterward assigned as the reason for not doing so, that he had incurred the enmity of the Indians by saving the life of Mr. Spalding, and had been detained a virtual prisoner for two or three weeks in Young Chief's camp.

I can find no evidence confirmatory of this statement, but much to the contrary. Mr. Gray* says:

"The women that lived through that terrible scene inform us that the priest was as familiar and friendly with the Indians as though nothing serious had occurred. We have seen and conversed freely with four of these unfortunate victims, and all affirm the same thing. Their impression was, that there might be others he expected to be

* *Oregon*, p. 491.

killed, and he did not wish to be present when it was done. According to the testimony in the case, Mr. Kimball and James Young were killed while he was at or near the station."

Besides, this story of the enmity of the Indians to Brouillet for sparing Spalding's life seems inconsistent with the claims made elsewhere by both Blanchet and Brouillet, that they were instrumental through their influence with the Indians, in saving the lives of others, and, with the aid of the Hudson Bay Company, of finally rescuing the survivors from their captors. We are aware, as a matter of fact, that the priests were prominent in the council held for this purpose with the Indians; we doubt not that their advice was in favor of the release of the women and children, and that it had great weight with the murderers. But while this shows their humanity after the massacre, and when the missionaries were no longer in their way, it shows also their influence over the Indians, and that the peril alleged could have had no better foundation than a very active imagination. In other words, such evidence proves too much, and leaves the reader to ask: If these priests and the Company had such great influence over these Indians, why did they not exert it before, and at least warn the missionaries and the American settlers of their danger?

Mrs. Victor pertinently inquires :*

"By what means did the Catholic priests procure perfect exemption from harm? Was it that they were French, and that they came into the country only as missionaries of a religion adapted to the savage mind, and not as

* *River of the West*, p. 419.

settlers? Was it fear that restrained them from showing sympathy? Certain it is, that they preserved a neutral position, when to be neutral was to seem, if not to be, devoid of human sympathies."

The claim is made for Brouillet that he was profoundly grieved and shocked at the sight of the victims, and assisted in the burial of the dead. No one will question that such were his feelings, or that he insisted on having the slain buried. And that, under such circumstances, this may have been very imperfectly done, we can readily believe. Respecting the manner of burial Mrs. Victor says:*

"The friends and acquaintances of Dr. Whitman were shocked to find that the remains of the victims [of the massacre] were still unburied, although a little earth had been thrown over them. Meek, to whom ever since his meeting with her in the train of the fur trader, Mrs. Whitman had seemed all that was noble and captivating, had the melancholy satisfaction of bestowing, with others, the last sad rite of burial upon such portions of her once fair person as murder and the wolves had not destroyed."

Our sole purpose in referring to this matter is, that Mr. Spalding in one of his statements speaks of the graves as having been torn open by wild beasts, leaving the bodies exposed. For so doing, he is described by the writer in the *Catholic World* as going "down to the grave at an old age with a load of falsehood and forgeries on his soul." A good cause and a valid defense is in no need of such vituperative language as this.

The accusation that the priests and the agents of the

* *River of the West*, p. 433.

Hudson Bay Company did not exhibit proper and humane feeling toward the survivors of the massacre, rests upon four well-defined charges:

I. That, although they knew of the threatened evils to the missionaries, and had almost unbounded influence over the Indians, the massacre was not only not prevented, but care was taken that the whites should not be warned of their peril. The evidence of this has been briefly presented already and need not be repeated.

II. That Mr. Hall, a mechanic, and a resident and employé at Dr. Whitman's station, was inhumanly treated.

According to Mr. Spalding's account of the massacre, in the Senate document:

"Four Indians attacked Mr. Hall lying on the floor in the cook room; the first gun missed fire, when Mr. Hall wrenched the gun from the Indian, and they ran, giving him time to reach the brush, where he lay till dark, and that night found his way to Fort Walla Walla, but was turned out, put over the Columbia River, and has never been heard from since. It is said he was immediately killed by the Indians. There were in the fort, besides the gentlemen in charge, some twenty white men, including some ten Catholic priests, who had arrived in the country about six weeks before, under the immediate superintendency of Bishop Blanchet and Vicar-General Brouillet, a part via Cape Horn and part by the overland route."

Of Mr. Hall's treatment by the agent of the Hudson Bay Company after his escape from the Indians, and his seeking protection at Fort Walla Walla, Mr. Gray says: "Mr. Hall was put across the Columbia River by McBean's order, and was lost, starved to death, or murdered by the Indians, we know not which."

We have another account of Mr. Hall's reception at the fort, on page 76 of Brouillet's pamphlet, where it is said that "he was received in Mr. McBean's private or family room," and, being "undecided whether to remain or proceed to the Willamette," 125 miles distant, he consulted with Mr. McBean and concluded that he could reach that place in safety. Before setting out "he was furnished with a cappo, blanket, powder, ball and tobacco, and Mr. McBean saw him safely across the river."

What value is to be attached to this statement, as confronted with those which Messrs. Spalding and Gray have given, each reader must decide for himself. It seems strange that a wounded man should think of undertaking so long and perilous a journey, if he had received hospitable treatment at the fort, and felt secure there; and it would have been much more to the advantage of McBean's reputation to detain him where he could be protected and kept in safety, instead of advising him to pursue such a wilderness journey. Mrs. Victor, writing of this same event, says: "Mr. Hall was received into the fort coldly, and remained there twelve hours; and hearing that all the captives were killed, owing to Mr. McBean's coldness proceeded on his way."

III. The same inhuman treatment, though not leading to the same fatal result, is charged as having been shown to the Osborne family.

We have an account of Mr. Osborne's escape from the Indians at the time of the murder, as given by himself on pages 31 and 32 of the Senate document, which we will abridge: "As the guns fired and the yells commenced, I leaned my head upon the bed and committed myself and family to my Maker. My wife removed the loose floor. I dropped under the floor and pulled it over us. In five minutes the room was full of Indians, but they did not discover us." He then describes the "yells of the savages," and "the groans of the dying;" and states that the family remained until dark in their place of concealment, when he, his children and his very feeble wife* "bent their steps toward Fort Walla Walla. The Indians were dancing a scalp-dance around a large fire at a distance. There seemed no hope for us, and we knew not which way to go. A dense, cold fog shut out every star, and the darkness was complete. We could see no trail, and not even the hand before the face."

Mr. Osborne describes the sufferings of himself and family while lying concealed in the brush, without food and exposed to the cold and rain, from Monday until Thursday morning, when with one child he reached Fort Walla Walla, and begged Mr. McBean for horses, food and clothing to bring his family in. "Mr. McBean," he says, "told me I could not bring my family to his fort. Mr. Hall had come in on Monday night, but he could not have an American in his fort, and he had put him over the Columbia River; that he could not let me have horses, or anything for my wife and children, and I must go to Umatilla. Insisted on bringing my family to the fort, but he refused; said he would not let us in. I next begged the priests to show pity, as my wife and children must perish, and the Indians would undoubtedly kill me; but with no

* They had all been sick with measles.

better success. I then begged to leave my child, who was now safe in the fort, but they refused."

Providentially, Mr. Stanley, an artist, had just arrived at the fort. He offered his horses to Mr. Osborne, who, with an Indian guide furnished by the agent, started back for his family on Thursday night, with a supply of food and clothing. After a long and perilous search he found them alive, and by the skill and fidelity of the guide they were saved from the Indians who sought their destruction. They started for the Umatilla, as McBean had ordered; but the guide, knowing their great danger from the lurking savages and Mrs. Osborne's feeble condition,* advised them to return to the fort. This they finally concluded to do. Reaching the fort late Sunday night—let us quote Mr. Osborne:

"I laid my wife down and knocked at the gate. Mr. McBean came and asked who was there. I replied. He said he could not let us in; we must go to Umatilla, or he would put us over the river, as he had Mr. Hall. My wife replied, that she would die at the gate, but she would not leave. He finally opened the gate and took us into a secret room, and sent an allowance of food for us every day. Next day I asked him for blankets for my sick wife to lie on. He had nothing. Next day I urged again. He had nothing to give, but would sell a blanket out of the store. I told him I had lost everything, and had nothing to pay, but if I should live to get to the Willamette, I would pay."

Brouillet, as usual, attempts to excuse or extenuate the conduct of the priests on the ground of their own extreme

---

* Mr. Eells tells us that she had to be tied to the Indian in order to be able to ride at all.

poverty, and of McBean on the plea that "provisions were very scarce at the time in the fort." He says that McBean did finally let Mr. Osborne have "a blanket on his credit," but passes over in silence his refusal to let the latter bring his family to the fort, and his ordering them to the Umatilla, where they were in imminent peril from lurking savages.

In a review of this treatment of Osborne by the agent of the Hudson Bay Company, Rev. Mr. Eells, than whom there is nowhere to be found a more lenient and just critic, says: "Why this Roman Catholic man in charge of the fort should do this, is absolutely known only to himself, but the appearances from his acts are that he intended to help on the murders."

And Mrs. Victor, in her *River of the West*, page 415, says of Mr. McBean:

"Whether it was from cowardice, or cruelty as some alleged, that Mr. McBean rejoiced in the slaughter of the Protestant missionaries, himself being a Catholic, can never be known. He refused shelter to Hall, a wounded man; and also refused Mr. Osborne horses to bring his wife and children to the fort, and food, and forbade his return to Fort Walla Walla. 'It is certain that some base and cowardly motive made him exceedingly cruel to both Hall and Osborne.' When Stanley, the artist, offered his horses to bring in his sick wife and children, McBean became ashamed of his base and cruel conduct, and subsequently furnished Osborne a guide to the Umatilla."

IV. The most serious charge, particularly as respects the conduct of the Romish priests, was their refusal to protect Miss Bewley from the criminal assaults of one of the Indian chiefs. Ten days after the massacre she was removed to the station on the Umatilla River which the priests had taken possession of only a few days before the murder. There Five Crows demanded her for his wife. The priests are accused of having, through fear or for some other cause, advised her to accompany the Indian to his lodge at night and afterward refused to let her remain in their house.

This is so grave a charge that we need all the information that can be produced. Necessarily the testimony must be confined to the parties present—the accused and the victim. We quote Vicar-General Brouillet's account, as given in the *Catholic World* of February, 1872.

"'We did,' says the reverend gentleman, 'all that charity could claim, and even more than prudence seemed to permit. We kept her for seventeen days in our house, provided for all her wants, and treated her well, and if she had minded us, and heeded our advice and entreaties, she would never have been subjected to that Indian. When she came first to our house, and told us that Five Crows had sent for her to be his wife, we asked her what she wanted to do. Did she want to go with him, or not? She said she did not want to go with him. Stay with us, then, if you like; we will do for you what we can, was our offer. When the evening came, the Indian chief called for her. The writer then requested his interpreter to tell him that she did not want to be his wife, and that, therefore, he did not want her to go with him. The interpreter, who was an Indian, allied by marriage to the Cayuses, and knew the chief's disposition well, would not provoke his anger, and refused to interpret. The writer, then making use of a few

Indian words he had picked up during the few days he had been there, and with the aid of signs, spoke to the Indian himself, and succeeded in making him understand what he meant. The Indian rose furiously, and without uttering a word went away. The young woman then got frightened and wanted to go for fear he might come back and do us all an injury. The writer tried to quiet her, and insisted that she should remain at our house, but to no avail; she must go, and off she went. The Indian, still in his fit of anger, refused to receive her, and sent her back. She remained with us three or four days undisturbed; until one evening, without any violence on the part of the Indian, or without advising with us, she went with him to his lodge. She came back the next morning, went off again in the evening, and continued so, without being forced by the Indian, and part of the time going by herself, until at last she was told to select between the Indian's lodge and our house, as such a loose way of acting could not be suffered any longer. That was the first and only time that she offered any resistance to the will of the Indian; but, indeed, her resistance was very slight, if we can believe her own statement."

As Miss Bewley's deposition is very extended, and covers other points besides the one under consideration, we will condense it, only giving in her own language what directly pertains to the priests' conduct. Those who wish to read the entire testimony are referred to the Senate document. The testimony was taken before a Justice of the Peace at Oregon City, December 12, 1848.

Miss Bewley was, like other helpless women and girls, subjected to the brutalities of the murderers while she remained at Waiilatpu. After an interval of ten days, during which she was repeatedly outraged by the Indians, she was taken to the Umatilla by an Indian who had been sent from that place for this purpose. To convey her, he brought with him a horse which Mr. Spalding had left in charge of Father Brouillet's interpreter when he made his escape. Though very sick from an attack of fever and ague, and so feeble that she had to be helped to mount the horse, Miss Bewley was obliged to accompany the Indian. The weather was extremely cold, and, without any shelter, she was compelled to pass the night with only a single blanket to protect her from the frozen earth. She reached Umatilla the morning after leaving Dr. Whitman's former station, and was met on her arrival by the Indian chief, who carried her, more dead than alive, into his lodge. He spread down robes and blankets and laid her upon them, and prepared food for her, which she was unable to eat. After her fever had passed off and she had rested, the chief told her she might go over to the white men's house, and that he would call for her at night. In the Bishop's house there were six white men—the Bishop, three priests and two Frenchmen. She states in her deposition that when she went there she "begged and cried to the Bishop for protection, either at his house, or to be sent to Walla Walla. I told him I would do any work by night and day for him if he would protect me. He said he would do all he could. .... The first night the Five Crows came, I refused to go, and he went away, apparently mad, and the Bishop told me I would better go, as he might do us all an injury, and the Bishop sent an Indian with me. He took me to the Five Crows lodge. The Five Crows showed me the door, and told me I might go back, and take my clothes, which I did. . . . . Three nights after this, the Five Crows came for me again. The Bishop finally ordered me to go; my answer was, I would rather die. After this, he still insisted on my going, as the best thing I could do. I was then in the Bishop's room; the three priests were there. I found I could get no help, and had to go, as he told me, out of his room. The Five Crows seized me by the arm and jerked me away to his lodge."

Miss Bewley adds that some days afterward, as Father Brouillet was about to start for Walla Walla, "he called me out of the door and told me if I went to the lodge any more I must not come back to his house. I asked him what I should do. He said I must insist or beg of the Indian to let me stop at his house; if he would not let me, then I must stop at his lodge." She then recounts a scene which took place that same night in the Bishop's house, when the Five Crows came and dragged her from her bed, to take her to his lodge, and adds: "I told the Frenchman to go into the Bishop's room and ask him what I should do; he came out and told me that the Bishop said it was best for me to go. I told him the tall priest said, if I went I must not come back again to this house; he said the priests dared not keep women about their house, but if the Five Crows sent me back again, why come. I still would not go. The Indian then pulled me away violently, without bonnet or shawl. Next morning I came back, and was in much anguish and cried much. The Bishop asked me if I was in much trouble. I told him I was. He said it was not my fault, that I could not help myself."*

After more than a fortnight of this abuse, Miss Bewley,

* Gray's *Oregon*, pp. 497-499.

with the surviving captives, was redeemed, the ransom being furnished by the Hudson Bay Company.

Rev. J. S. Griffin testifies to the correctness of the above statement, as having been made by Miss Bewley; and others have given depositions confirming it in many respects; but from the nature of the case there was no living person who could verify the most of her testimony.

It is claimed, by those who would exculpate the priests, that Miss Bewley made a later statement, quoted in the Senate document, differing from this in giving more particulars of one or two of the scenes in the tragic history. This difference has been made the occasion of accusing Mr. Spalding of altering her statement to suit his own purposes. This charge will have little weight with those who knew Mr. Spalding, and were acquainted with his manner of life and his work. Its weakness is especially apparent in the light of the fact that such men as Governor Abernethy, Commissary-General Palmer, Indian Agent J. W. Anderson, Chief Justice Hewet, Surveyor-General Garfielde, Secretaries Evans and Smith, and hundreds of others, residents of Oregon, to say nothing of all the religious bodies in that country, as late as 1865, memorialized the governor of Idaho, to appoint Mr. Spalding Superintendent of Instruction, and testified to his great moral worth and his superior qualifications for the important duties of the office.

We find the following in Mrs. Victor's *River of the West*, page 422; it shows her impression of the facts as they had come within her knowledge:

"To this house (the Bishop's) Miss Bewley applied for protection, and was refused, whether from fear, or from the motives subsequently attributed to them by some Protestant writers in Oregon, is not known to any but themselves. The only thing certain about it is, that Miss Bewley was allowed to be violently dragged from their presence every night to return to them weeping in the morning, and to have her entreaties for their assistance answered by assurances from them that the wisest course for her was to submit. And this continued for more than two weeks, until the news of Mr. Ogden's arrival at Walla Walla became known, when Miss Bewley was told that if Five Crows would not allow her to remain at their house altogether, she must remain at the lodge of Five Crows without coming to their house at all, well knowing what Five Crows would do, but wishing to have Miss Bewley's action seem voluntary, from shame, perhaps, at their own cowardice.''

With this testimony from Mrs. Victor, we leave the matter to the candid verdict of our readers. As she is quoted by Roman Catholics to prove that it was Dr. Whitman's imprudence, if not double-dealing, which excited the Indians and led to the final outbreak of hostilities, and that the Protestant missions had resulted in comparatively little benefit to the Cayuse and Nez Percé tribes, they cannot take exception to her value as a witness. To say the least, her opportunities of information on this topic were as good as on the others ; nor can she be accused of hostility to the priests or of partiality for the missionaries.

CHAPTER XIV.

OREGON SAVED TO THE UNITED STATES.

IN closing this review it is desirable to present some additional facts about Dr. Whitman's patriotic services in behalf of the settlement of Oregon by American citizens, and its ultimate control by our government. This is the more fitting since some late writers have not hesitated to deny that his visit to the East in 1842–43 had any such purpose in view, and to declare that his sole object was to induce the American Board not to discontinue its missions among the Indians on the Pacific Coast, or curtail the operations and expenditures of the missionaries, as it had been disposed to do owing to the failure of the missions to fulfill anticipations.

All questions on this head should forever be set at rest by the following explicit statement taken from the *Missionary Herald* of Boston, the official organ of the American Board of Commissioners for Foreign Missions.

"While it is apparent from the letters of Dr. Whitman at the Missionary House, that in visiting the Eastern States in 1842–43, he had certain missionary objects in view,* it is no less clear that he would not have come at that time, and probably would not have come at all, had it not been his desire to save the disputed territory to the United

---

* One of these was a large increase of helpers, for which purpose Mr. Gray had been previously sent to the East.

States. It was not simply an American question, however; it was at the same time a Protestant question. He was fully alive to the efforts which the Roman Catholics were making to gain the mastery on the Pacific Coast, and he was firmly persuaded that they were working in the interest of the Hudson Bay Company, with a view to this very end. The danger from this quarter had made a profound impression upon his mind. Under date of April 1, 1847, he wrote: 'In the autumn of 1842, I pointed out to our mission the arrangements of the Papal priests to settle in our vicinity, and that it only required that those arrangements should be completed to close our operations.'"

Dr. William Geiger recalls many conversations with Dr. Whitman on the object of his going, and that "his main object was to save the country to the United States, as he believed there was great danger of its falling into the hands of England. Incidentally he intended to obtain more missionary help."

Testimony as direct and equally explicit is borne by Rev. Mr. Spalding, Rev. C. Eells, Hon. A. L. Lovejoy, his companion on the winter journey, Mr. Perrin B. Whitman, his nephew, Hon. Alanson Hinman, and Samuel J. Parker, M.D., son of the pioneer missionary of the American Board's missions in Oregon. These all affirm in substance that the perilous trip was undertaken "to prevent, if possible, the trading off of this northwest coast to the British government," and, as a means to this end, "the bringing of an immigration of American settlers across the plains."

As further showing Dr. Whitman's relations to the American Board and the reasons for his journey, we fortunately have a letter written by him to the Board, April 1, 1847, in which he says:

"American interests acquired in the country, which the success of the immigration of 1843 alone did and could have secured, have become the foundation of the late treaty between England and the United States in regard to Oregon; for it may easily be seen what would have become of American interests in this country had the results of that immigration been as disastrous as have been the two attempts in 1845 and 1846 to alter the route then followed. Any one may see that American interests, as now acquired, have had more to do in securing the treaty than our original rights. From 1835 till now it has been apparent that there was a choice of only two things: (1) The increase of British interests to the exclusion of all other rights in the country, or (2) the establishment of American interests by citizens on the ground. In the fall of 1842 I pointed out to our mission the arrangements of the Papists to settle here, which might oblige us to retire. This was urged as a reason why I should return home and try to bring out men to carry on the secular work of the missionary stations, and others to settle in the country on the footing of citizens and not as missionaries. You will please receive this as an explanation of many of my measures and much of my policy."

Mr. Gray, the secular agent of the mission, confirms the above statement. "We can bear positive testimony," he says, "that Dr. Whitman did point out to his associates all the dangers to which they were exposed."

An article in the *Congregationalist*, of Boston, by a writer familiar with this subject, sums up the evidence by stating:

"Dr. Whitman evidently regarded his visit to Washington, and his success in conducting 875 emigrants across the Rocky Mountains, as settling the destiny of Oregon."

In the face of all this evidence, nothing but an invincible prejudice will account for the refusal of some persons still to recognize the patriotic services rendered by Dr. Whitman, and their denial even that he was in Washington during his visit to the East in the spring of 1843; though Rev. Drs. Barrows and Hale, of St. Louis; Judge James Otis, of Chicago, and Governor Ramsey, of Minnesota, all testify to having met and conversed with him respecting his interviews with Daniel Webster, the President, and the Cabinet, Hubert H. Bancroft, in his history of Oregon, entirely ignores Dr. Whitman's visit to Washington and his services there in behalf of Oregon.

Happily for the truth of history and the vindication of a great and good man, evidence has come to light that absolutely settles the fact of Dr. Whitman's presence in Washington, and of his repeated interviews with the heads of the government respecting the Northwest Territory. Among the documents in the War Department there are two, discovered recently, written by Dr. Whitman, and addressed to Hon. James M. Porter, Secretary of War in 1843 under President Tyler. The one is a bill prepared by him, and which he proposed Congress should pass, "to promote safe intercourse with the territory of Oregon; to suppress violent acts of aggression on the part of certain Indian tribes; the better to protect the revenue; and for the transportation of the mail, and other purposes." The act provides for establishing agricultural posts or farming stations from the Kansas River to the settlements of the Willamette in

Oregon; that at each of these there shall reside a superintendent and a deputy superintendent, "having charge and power to carry into effect the provisions of this act, subject to the instructions of the President;" and that there shall also be laborers and artificers, not exceeding twenty, whose appointment and dismissal shall rest with the superintendent.

It further provides for suitable buildings, supplied with necessary mechanical and agricultural implements; "that at each post, not to exceed 640 acres of land be cultivated with products there required; that the superintendents shall be appointed by the President, and hold office four years, who are to make an annual statement to the Secretary of the Treasury of all receipts and disbursements. They shall have charge of the Indians under the control of the Commissioner-General of Indian Affairs; have power to administer oaths and to act as civil magistrates, with authority to arrest all disorderly white persons, and to punish Indians committing acts against the laws of the United States; and finally to act as postmasters at their stations, but without compensation."

In explanation and advocacy of this bill, prepared and sent to the Secretary of War, Dr. Whitman accompanied it with a letter of more than ten pages, closely written. The letter is of such importance in vindicating the truth of history, that we print it as an appendix to this volume.

These documents forever settle the dispute respecting Dr. Whitman's presence in Washington in the spring of 1843, the importance of the information he conveyed, and the plan which he submitted to the Cabinet of President Tyler for the maintenance of our Oregon possessions. His information was needed and was welcomed, and his plan to save Oregon was adopted.

In the New York *Independent* of January, 1870, we are told that "A personal friend of Mr. Webster (then Secretary of State), a legal gentleman, and with whom he conversed on the subject, several times remarked, 'It is safe to assert that our country owes it to Dr. Whitman and his associate missionaries that all of the territory west of the Rocky Mountains, and south as far as the Columbia River, is not owned by England and held by the Hudson Bay Company.'"

And Dr. Barrows, in his *History of Oregon and the Struggle for Possession*, says sententiously and truly that "American enterprise, pioneered by American missionaries, secured Oregon to the United States."

So far as known, Dr. Whitman's bill did not get before Congress. Probably before this could be done Mr. Porter ceased to be Secretary of War, as the Senate failed to confirm his nomination.

In presenting the timely and valuable services of Dr. Whitman to his country at this period when the possession of Oregon was to be decided, I avail myself of the clear and candid statement of the condition of the territory, by Rev. Dr. S. H. Willey,* of San Francisco, Cal., in the *Pacific* of September 2, 1885. There could hardly be found on the Pacific Coast a person better informed than he, or one whose representation would carry a stronger or more general conviction of the truth to all unprejudiced minds.

The article first deals with the difficulties which the

* An honored minister and early resident on the Pacific Coast.

Protestant missionaries encountered, owing to the intrusion of Papal priests upon their field of labor, with the approval and aid of the Hudson Bay Company, when at once " the most persistent exertions were used, both secret and open, to turn away the natives from the instruction " of their former Protestant mission teachers, leading to anxiety and discouragement lest the hard work of four years should be interrupted, if not wholly destroyed. This was followed in the early part of 1842 by a revival among the Indians of their interest in the Protestant missions, leading the missionaries to prosecute their labors with increased vigor, and with correspondingly gratifying and beneficial results.

The article proceeds then to speak more specifically of Dr. Whitman and his services for Oregon:

"As the autumn of 1842 came on, a new subject of anxiety presented itself. Immigrants arrived from across the Rocky Mountains, bringing the news that the long-pending 'Oregon question' was coming to a settlement. The critical issue was on the eve of decision—which flag was to wave over this great Northwest, that of Great Britain or that of the United States. It was not, in fact, so near to a decision as the news at this time indicated : but it stirred up the anxiety of what few inhabitants there were in Oregon, on both sides, to fever heat. From all that could be learned, it was believed by our missionaries that the decision was coming on without the real facts being known as to the vast value of the country. Dr. Whitman, especially, felt this keenly. From four or five years' observation he had become profoundly convinced of its immense value for homes for a great people, rather than as the hunting-ground for a foreign fur-trading monopoly. He knew what exertions the Hudson Bay Company were making to retain the territory, and what vigor they inspired in the British government to insist on its right to it. And he did not think that our own United States government was fully informed of the value of the country they were negotiating about. And it would seem, in reading their speeches in the light of to-day, that our public men, even at a later day, knew very little indeed of it."

In support of this view, the writer quotes from the speeches of Senators Dayton, of New Jersey, and McDuffie, of South Carolina, and from the opinion of Mr. Webster, as recorded in his works, Vol. i, p. 149, and Vol. v, p. 102. As these have been referred to elsewhere in this volume, they do not require to be here quoted.

"Is it strange, then," the writer asks, "that Dr. Whitman was stirred by an immense anxiety when he understood, from news just received,* that the ownership of all Oregon was on the eve of being decided—decided, too, in such utter ignorance, on the part of our statesmen, of its real value? The rightfulness of the claim of the United States to the country was admitted and believed in by all parties, as the opposite was believed in by the British; but its worth seemed to be held in such low esteem that there appeared to be almost a willingness to abandon it. Dr. Whitman, on the contrary, had lived in Oregon several years. He had tested its soil. He had observed its climate. He had traveled in it many thousand miles. He knew that it was capable of sustaining a great population. He knew, too, as very few other men did know, that wagon-trains with men, women and children could come all the

* Brought by immigration party, fall of 1842.

way from the East across the Rocky Mountains to this productive and genial country. He knew that the competing claims of Great Britain and the United States were so evenly balanced that the fact of the actual settlement of the country by either party would mainly determine the ownership. He saw the beginning of a competing settlement in the Red River emigration from the British Northeast, some hundred or two persons, and he observed the exultation with which their coming was greeted. To his mind the moment was critical. Whatever was done to determine the future must be done instantly. Two keys must be touched—one the key of diplomacy, as against bartering the Oregon claim for any equivalent; the other the key of actual occupation, planting American homes in abundance on the rich lands in Oregon, while yet the country was open to joint occupation. But if he would touch these keys, he must do it at the East. No wires then connected this coast with Washington, or the great West from which immigration could be looked for. How could he reach the East? It is now October. The news just received leads him to think that whatever information shall avail anything at Washington must reach the government immediately; and whatever is done to stimulate the next year's emigration must be done before spring. How could he get there? The journey was hard enough in the best season of the year and in the protecting company of a caravan. How powerful the motive that could nerve a man, who knew so well the perils of mountain travel, to undertake such a journey alone, and in the winter? But such a motive the Oregon situation applied to Dr. Whitman's mind. Against the remonstrance of his friends and associates, he determines to attempt the journey. One attendant alone accompanies him; it is A. L. Lovejoy, who had just arrived overland with the small immigration of 1842, and brought the information concerning Oregon matters at the East that so stirred Dr. Whitman. On October 3, 1842, they mount, and are off for an attempt to reach the Eastern States before spring.

"Through storms and snows, in spite of hunger and fatigue, they made their lonely way through regions traversed only by savages and wild beasts, climbing mountains and swimming rivers, from the ice-bound border of the swift current on the one side to the ice-bound border on the other side. By a circuitous southern route *they at last reached St. Louis* late in the month of February, 1843. Hastening on to Washington, Dr. Whitman did what he could for Oregon with the government, and then made his way to Boston and arranged the affairs of the mission with the American Board, and was back in the West in season to join the great decisive emigration of the year 1843, that really settled the 'Oregon question.' This emigration consisted of nearly a thousand persons. Dr. Whitman did all that he possibly could, by speech and pen, during the short time he was East, to stimulate the emigration and awaken an interest in Oregon. And, although he found that the actual settlement of the boundary line between England and the United States was not as near as he had been led to suppose, the preliminary step toward it was soon taken, by the year's notice given in 1844 of the termination of the 'joint occupation.'"

Of Dr. Whitman's services to the cause while at Washington, we append only two or three brief additional statements. Says Hon. Elwood Evans:

"There is no doubt that the arrival of Dr. Whitman was opportune. The President was satisfied that the territory was worth the effort to save it. The delay incident to the transfer of negotiations to London was fortunate."

In an article printed in the New York *Observer* in 1883, Dr. Barrows, the author of the history of Oregon in the American Commonwealth series, says:

"The Doctor had arrived in Washington just in time to make such a visit of the greatest service in weakening the English and strengthening the American claims. His information supplemented that of the President, Secretary, and Congress generally; and it rectified the wrong impressions and unjust bias which English statements had made, and it exposed the bold scheme of the Hudson Bay Company to capture the territory by stealthy colonization; and to him above any other man, and beyond comparison, must be given the credit of saving Oregon."

Mr. H. O. Lang, the author of a valuable history of the Willamette Valley, page 266, thus writes:

"No one can have read the preceding pages without having become convinced of the sterling integrity, firmness of purpose, and energy of action of Doctor Whitman. His character and services to the American cause entitle him to the first place among those whose memory the citizens of Oregon should ever revere, and whom all true Americans should honor. It has settled beyond dispute, in the minds of those who have given the subject a just and careful consideration, the permanent and exalted position

Doctor Whitman must ever occupy in the annals of Oregon."

In *The Advance* of March 14, 1895, is this tribute:

"Is there in history the record of a man who by himself saved for his country so vast and so valuable a territory as did Whitman by his prophetic heroism of 1842–43? . . . . His ride across the continent in the winter of 1842, a winter memorable for its severity, is without a parallel in history. It stands as the sublime achievement of a prophet and a hero, who saw and suffered that his country might gain. The United States paid $10,000,000 for Alaska. It bought Louisiana for millions more. It paid a Mexican War, blood and money, for the acquisition of Texas and New Mexico. But what did it pay for Washington and Oregon and Idaho, a territory into which New England and the Middle States might be put, with Maryland, Virginia, West Virginia and three Connecticuts? It paid not one cent. That vast region cost the Nation nothing. It cost it only the sufferings and perils of Marcus Whitman, who risked his life and endured all hardships that the territory of his adoption might belong to the country of his birth."

Again, in the same number of that paper, we find the following :

"Marcus Whitman was one of the splendid heroes and benefactors of the Republic. . . . . What he did for the Nation, through his clear insight into the motives and aims of men, whose loyalty was to another flag than the stars and stripes, and by his prompt action, brave sacrifices and unfaltering determination, in saving an imperial and priceless section of our domain to be a part of the United

States, had he been a soldier or a politician, would have made his name a household word from end to end of our vast Commonwealth."

We close this volume, itself a labor of love, by a brief and touching tribute from the pen of Rev. H. K. Hines, of Fort Vancouver, in the present State of Washington, who was personally acquainted with Dr. Whitman and fully aware of his comprehensive views, and of his devotion to the cause of Christian missions:

"On the banks of the Walla Walla, in a lowly grave, unmarked by an inscription, the mortal remains of Dr. and Mrs. Whitman are slumbering away the years. They sleep not far from the spot where the consecrated years of their mature life were so lavishly given to that noblest of all work, raising the fallen and saving the lost. Living, they were the peers of such a hero and heroine as Dr. and Mrs. Judson; and dying, their memory is entitled to the same enshrinement in the grateful regards of a church and state, indebted to them for one of the finest illustrations of unselfish patriotism and of the purity and power of ancient faith. And when he whom they served with such special devotion shall assemble his best beloved, they of the eastern shall greet those of the western shore of the Pacific, and hail them fellow-heirs to martyr's robe and crown."

APPENDIX.

To the Hon. James M. Porter, *Secretary of War:*

Sir: In compliance with the request you did me the honor to make last winter while at Washington, I herewith transmit you the synopsis of a bill which, if it could be adopted, would, according to my experience and observation, prove highly conducive to the best interests of the United States generally, to Oregon, where I have resided for more than seven years as a missionary, and to the Indian tribes that inhabit the intermediate country.

The Government will doubtless now for the first time be apprised through you, and by means of this communication, of the immense migration of families to Oregon which has taken place this year. I have since our interview been instrumental in piloting across the route described in the accompanying bill, and which is the only eligible wagon road, families consisting of no less than one thousand persons of both sexes, with their wagons, amounting in all to more than one hundred and twenty, 698 oxen and 173 loose cattle. The emigrants are from different States, but principally from Missouri, Arkansas, Illinois and New York. The majority of them are farmers, lured by the prospects of government bounty in lands, by the reported fertility of the soil, and by the desire to be first among those who are planting our institutions on the

Pacific Coast. Among them also are artisans of every trade, comprising with farmers the very best material for a new colony. As pioneers these people have undergone incredible hardships, and, having now safely passed the Blue Mountain range with their wagons and effects, have established a durable road from Missouri to Oregon, which will serve to mark permanently the route for large numbers each succeeding year, while they have practically demonstrated that wagons drawn by horses or oxen can cross the Rocky Mountains to the Columbia River, contrary to all the sinister assertions of those who pretended it to be impossible.

In their slow progress these persons have encountered, as in all former instances, and as all succeeding emigrants must, if this or some similar bill be not passed by Congress, the continued fear of Indian aggression, the actual loss through them of horses, cattle and other property, and the great labor of transporting an adequate amount of provisions for so long a journey. The bill herewith proposed would in a great measure lessen these inconveniences by the establishment of posts, which, while they possessed power to keep the Indians in check, thus doing away [with] the necessity of constant military vigilance on the part of the traveler by day and night, would be able to furnish them [emigrants] in transit with fresh supplies of provisions, diminish the original burdens of the emigrants, and finding thus a ready and profitable market for their produce, a market that would in my opinion more than suffice to defray all the current expenses of such posts. The present party are supposed to have expended no less than two thousand dollars at Laramie and Bridger Forts, and as much more at Fort Hall and at Fort Boisé, two of the Hudson Bay Company's stations. These are at present the only stopping places in a journey of twenty-two hundred miles, and the only places where additional supplies can be obtained even at the enormous rates of charge called mountain prices—fifty dollars the hundred for flour and fifty dollars the hundred for coffee, the same for sugar and powder, etc.

There were many cases of sickness and some deaths among those who accomplished the journey this season, owing in a great measure to the uninterrupted use of meat, salt and fresh, with flour, which constitute the chief articles of food they are able to convey in their wagons, and this would be obviated by the vegetable productions which the posts in contemplation could very profitably afford them. Those who rely upon hunting as an auxiliary support are at present unable to have their arms repaired when out of order; horses and oxen become tender-footed and require to be shod on their long journey, sometimes repeatedly, and the wagons must be repaired in a variety of ways. I mention these as valuable incidents to the proposed measure, as it will also be found to tend in many other incidental ways to benefit the migratory population of the United States choosing to take this direction, and on these accounts, as well as for the immediate use of the posts themselves, they ought to be provided with the necessary shops and mechanics, which would at the same time exhibit the several branches of civilized art to the Indians.

The outlay in the first instance need be but trifling. Forts like those of the Hudson Bay Company, surrounded by walls enclosing all the buildings, and constructed almost entirely of adobe or sun-dried bricks with stone foundations only, can be easily and cheaply erected. There are very eligible places for as many of these as the Government will find necessary, at suitable distances, not further than one or two hundred miles apart, at the main crossings of the principal streams which now form impediments to the journey, and consequently well supplied with water, having alluvial bottom lands of a rich quality and generally well wooded. If I might be allowed to suggest the best sites for said posts, my personal knowledge and observation enable me to recommend : First, the main crossing of the Kansas River, where a ferry would be very convenient to the traveler and profitable to the station having it in charge; next, and about eighty miles distant, the crossing of Blue River, where in times of an unusual freshet a ferry would be in like manner useful ; next, and distant from one hundred to one hundred and fifty miles from the last mentioned, the Little Blue or Republican fork of the Kansas ; next, and from sixty to one hundred miles distant from the last mentioned, the point of intersection of the Platte River; next, and from one hundred to one hundred and fifty miles distant from this, last mentioned, the crossing of the South Fork of Platte River ; next, and about one hundred and eighty or two hundred miles distant (from the last mentioned), Horse Shoe Creek, which is about forty miles west of Laramie's Fork in the Black Hills. There is a fine creek for mills and irrigation, good land for cultivation, fine pasturage and timber and stone for building. Other locations may be had along the Platte and Sweetwater, on the Green River, or Black or Hain's Fork on the

Bear River near the great Soda Springs; near Fort Hall, and at suitable places down to the Columbia. These localities are all of the best description, and so situated as to hold a ready intercourse with the Indians in their passage to and from the ordinary Buffalo hunting grounds; and in themselves so well situated in all other respects as to be desirable to private enterprise if the usual advantages of trade existed. Any of the farms above indicated would be deemed extremely valuable in the States.

The Government cannot long overlook the importance of superintending the savages who endanger this line of travel, and who are not yet in treaty with it. Some of these are already well-known to be led by desperate white men and mongrels, who form banditti in the most difficult passes, and at all times are ready to cut off some lagging emigrant in the rear of the party, or some adventurous one who may proceed a few miles in advance, or at night to make a descent upon the sleeping camp and carry away or kill horses and cattle. This is the case even now in the commencement of our western emigration, and when it comes to be more generally known that large quantities of valuable property and considerable sums of money are yearly carried over this desolate region, it is to be feared an organized banditti will be instituted. The posts in contemplation would effectually counteract this; for that purpose they need not, nor ought not to be military establishments. The trading posts in this country have never been of such a character, and yet with a very few men in them have for years kept the surrounding Indians in the most pacific disposition, so that the traveler feels secure from molestation upon approaching Fort Laramie, Bridger's

Fort, Fort Hall, etc. The same can be obtained without any considerable expenditure by the Government, while, by investing the officers in charge with competent authority, all evil-disposed white men, refugees from justice, or discharged vagabonds from the trading posts, might be easily removed from among the Indians and sent to the appropriate states for trial. The Hudson Bay Company's system of rewards among the savages would soon enable the posts to root out these desperadoes. A direct and friendly intercourse with all the tribes, even to the Pacific, might be thus maintained, the government would become more intimately acquainted with them, and they with the government; and, instead of sending to the state courts a manifestly guilty Indian to be arraigned before a distant tribunal, and acquitted for the want of testimony by the technicalities of lawyers and of laws unknown to them, and sent back into the wilderness loaded with presents as an inducement to further crime, the posts should be enabled to execute summary justice as if the criminal had been already condemned by his tribe, because the tribe will be sure to deliver up none but the party whom they know to be guilty. They will in that way receive the trial of their peers and secure within themselves, to all intents and purposes, if not technically the trial by jury, yet the spirit of that trial. There are many powers which ought to reside in some person on this extended route for the convenience and even necessity of the public.

In this the immigrants and the people of Oregon are no more interested than the resident inhabitants of the states. At present no person is authorized to administer an oath or legally attest a fact from the western line of Missouri to the Pacific. The immigrant cannot dispose of his property at home, although an opportunity ever so advantageous to him should occur, after he passes the western border of Missouri. No one can here make legal demand and protest of a promissory note or bill of exchange. No one can secure the valuable testimony of a mountaineer, or of our emigrating whites after he has entered this at present lawless country. Causes do exist and will continually arise in which the private rights of citizens are and will be seriously prejudiced by such an utter absence of legal authority. A contraband trade from Mexico, the introduction from that country of liquors to be sold among the Indians west of the Kansas River, is already carried on with the mountain trappers, and very soon the teas, silks, nankins, spices, camphor and opium of the East Indies will find their way, duty free, through Oregon, across the mountains and into the States, unless custom house officers along this line find an interest in intercepting them.

Your familiarity with the government policy, duties and interest, renders it unnecessary for me to more than hint at the several objects intended by the enclosed bill, and enlargement upon the topics here suggested as inducements to its adoption would be quite superfluous, if not impertinent. The very existence of such a system as the one above recommended, suggests the utility of post-office and mail arrangements, which it is the wish of all who now live in Oregon to have granted to them, and I need only add that contracts for this purpose will be readily taken at reasonable rates for transporting the mail across from Missouri to the mouth of the Columbia in forty days, with fresh horses at each of the contemplated posts. The ruling policy proposed regards the Indians as the police of the country, who are to be relied upon to keep the peace not only for themselves, but to expel lawless white men and prevent banditti, under the salutary guidance of the superintendents of the several posts, aided by a well-directed system of bounty, to induce the punishment of crime. It will be only after a failure of these means to procure the delivery or punishment of violent, lawless and savage acts of aggression, that a band or tribe should be regarded as conspirators against the peace, and punished accordingly by force of arms.

Hoping that these suggestions may meet your approbation, and conduce to the future interest of our growing colony, I have the honor to be, Honorable Sir,

Your obedient servant,
MARCUS WHITMAN.

WHITMAN'S RIDE.

BY ALICE WELLINGTON ROLLINS.

(After " Paul Revere.")

Listen, my children, and you shall hear
Of a hero's ride that saved a State.
A midnight ride? Nay, child, for a year
He rode with the message that could not wait.
Eighteen hundred and forty-two;
No railroad then had gone crashing through
To the Western coast; not a telegraph wire
Had guided there the electric fire;
But a fire burned in one strong man's breast
For a beacon-light. You shall hear the rest.

He said to his wife: "At the fort to-day,
At Walla Walla, I heard them say
That a hundred British men had crossed
The mountains; and one young, ardent priest
Shouted, 'Hurrah for Oregon!
The Yankees are late by a year at least!'
They must know this at once at Washington.
Another year and all would be lost.
Some one must ride, to give the alarm,
Across the continent; untold harm
In an hour's delay; and only I
Can make them understand how or why
The United States must keep Oregon!"

Twenty-four hours he stopped to think.
To think? Nay, then, if he thought at all,
He thought as he tightened his saddle-girth,
One tried companion, who would not shrink
From the worst to come; just a mule or two
To carry arms and supplies, would do,
With a guide as far as Fort Bent. And she,
The woman of proud heroic worth,
Who must part from him, if she wept at all,
Wept as she gathered whatever he
Might need for the outfit on his way.
Fame for the man who rode that day
Into the wilds at his country's call:
And for her who waited for him a year
On that wild Pacific coast, a tear!

Then he said "Good-bye!" and with firm-set lips
Silently rode from his cabin door,
Just as the sun rose over the tips
Of the phantom mountains that loomed before
The woman there in the cabin door,
With a dread at her heart she had not known
When she, with him, had dared to cross
The Great Divide. None better than she
Knew what the terrible ride would cost
As he rode, and she waited, each alone.
Whether all were gained or all were lost,
No message of either gain or loss
Could reach her; never a greeting stir
Her heart with sorrow or gladness; he
In another year would come back to her
If all went well; and if all went ill—
Ah, God! could even her courage still
The pain at her heart? If the blinding snow
Were his winding sheet, she would never know;

If the Indian arrow pierced his side,
She would never know where he lay and died;
If the icy mountain-torrents drowned
His cry for help, she would hear no sound!
Nay, none would hear, save God, who knew
What she had to bear, and she had to do.
The clattering hoof-beats died away
On the Walla Walla. Ah! had she known
They would echo in history still to-day
As they echoed then from her heart of stone!

He has left the valley. The mountains mock
His coming. Behind him, broad and deep,
The Columbia meets the Pacific tides.
Before him—four thousand miles before—
Four thousand miles from his cabin door,
The Potomac meets the Atlantic. On,
Over the trail grown rough and steep,
Now soft on the snow, now loud on the rock,
Is heard the tramp of his steed as he rides.
The United States must keep Oregon.

It was October when he left
The Walla Walla, though little heed
Paid he to the season. Nay, indeed,
In the lonely cañon just ahead,
Little mattered it what the almanacs said.
He heard the coyotes bark; but they
Are harmless creatures. No need to fear
A deadly rattlesnake coiled too near.
No rattlesnake ever was so bereft
Of sense as to creep out such a day
In the frost. Nay, scarce would a grizzly care
For a sniff at him. Only a man would dare

The bitter cold, in whose heart and brain
Burned the quenchless flame of a great desire—
A man with nothing himself to gain
From success, but whose heart blood kept its fire,
While with freezing face he rode on and on.
The United States must keep Oregon.

It was November when they came
To the icy stream. Would he hesitate?
Not he, the man who carried a State
At his saddle-bow. They have made the leap;
Horse and rider have plunged below
The icy current that could not tame
Their proud life-current's fiercer flow.
They swim for it, reach it, clutch the shore,
Climb the river-bank cold and steep,
Mount, and ride the rest of that day,
Cased in an armor close and fine
As ever an ancient warrior wore:
Armor of ice that dared to shine
Back at a sunbeam's dazzling ray,
Fearless as plated steel of old
Before the slender lance of gold!

It is December as they ride
Slowly across the Great Divide;
The blinding storm turns day to night,
And clogs their feet; the snowflakes roll
Their winding-sheet about them; sight
Is darkened; faint the despairing soul.
No trail before or behind them. Spur
His horse? Nay, child, it were death to stir!
Motionless horse and rider stand,
Turning to stone; till one poor mule,
Pricking his ears as if to say
If they gave him rein he would find the way,

Found it, and led them back, poor fool,
To last night's camp in that lonely land.

It was January when he rode
Into St. Louis. The gaping crowd
Gathered about with questions loud
And eager. He raised one frozen hand
With a gesture of silent, proud command:
"I am here to ask, not answer! Tell
Me quick, Is the treaty signed?" "Why, yes!
In August, six months ago, or less!"
Six months ago! Two months before
The gay young priest at the fortress showed
The English hand! Two months before,
Four months ago at his cabin door,
He had saddled his horse! Too late, then. "Well,
But Oregon? Have they signed the State
Away?" "Of course not. Nobody cares
About Oregon." He in silence bares
His head: "Thank God! I am not too late!"
It was March when he rode at last
Into the streets of Washington.
The warning questions came thick and fast:
"Do you know that the British will colonize,
If you wait another year, Oregon
And the Northwest, thirty-six times the size
Of Massachusetts!" A courteous stare,
And the Government murmurs: "Ah! indeed!
Pray, why do you think that we should care?
With Indian arrows and mountain snow
Between us, we never can colonize
The wild Northwest from the East, you know.
If you doubt it, why, we will let you read
The London Examiner; proofs enough.
The Northwest is worth just a pinch of snuff!"

And the Board of Missions that sent him out
Gazed at the worn and weary man
With stern displeasure: "Pray, sir, who
Gave you orders to undertake
This journey hither, or to incur,
Without due cause, such great expense
To the Board? Do you suppose we can
Overlook so grave an offense?
And the Indian converts? What about
The little flock for whose precious sake
We sent you west? Can it be that you
Left them without a shepherd? Most
Extraordinary conduct, sir,
Thus to desert your chosen post!"

Ah, well! What mattered it? He had dared
A hundred deaths in his eager pride
To bring to his country at Washington
A message for which, then, no one cared!
But Whitman could act, as well as ride;
The United States must keep the Northwest.
He—whatever might say the rest—
Cared, and would colonize Oregon!

It was October, forty-two,
When the clattering hoof-beats died away
On the Walla Walla, that fateful day.
It was September, forty-three—
Little less than a year, you see—
When the woman who waited, thought she heard
The clatter of hoof-beats that she knew
On the Walla Walla again. "What word
From Whitman?" Whitman himself! And see!
What do her glad eyes look upon?

The first of two hundred wagons rolls
Into the valley before her. He
Who, a year ago, had left her side,
Had brought them over the Great Divide—
Men, women and children, a thousand souls—
The Army to occupy Oregon.

You know the rest. In the books you have read
That the British were not a year ahead.
The United States have kept Oregon
Because of one Marcus Whitman. He
Rode eight thousand miles, and was not too late!
In his single hand, not a Nation's fate
Perhaps; but a gift for the Nation she
Would hardly part with to-day, if we
May believe what the papers say upon
This great Northwest that was Oregon.

And Whitman! Ah! my children, he
And his wife sleep now in a martyr's grave!
Murdered! Murdered both he and she,
By the Indian souls they went West to save!
—*From Representative Poems, Cassell & Co., New York.*

www.ingramcontent.com/pod-product-compliance
Lightning Source LLC
Chambersburg PA
CBHW020901230426
43666CB00008B/1268